by Charles Evers

Edited and with an Introduction by Grace Halsell

The World Publishing Company
New York and Cleveland

For Medgar

Published by The World Publishing Company
Published simultaneously in Canada
by Nelson, Foster & Scott Ltd.
First printing—1971
Copyright © 1971 by Charles Evers and Grace Halsell
All rights reserved
Library of Congress catalog card number: 74-142136
Designed by Jacques Chazaud
Printed in the United States of America
WORLD PUBLISHING
TIMES MIRROR

Introduction

Before knowing him, I naïvely imagined Charles Evers to be a turn-the-other-cheek American soul brother of Mahatma Gandhi. In my mind's eye he was a selfless mendicant who, having given all his worldly goods to the poor, was out saving souls, and if you were to scratch him ever so slightly you would find not blood and bone but goodness and mercy.

I was wrong. Evers is in every sense a man of his people, a slightly refined product of a raw environment. He is neither saintly nor supine. And if anyone slapped his face, he would, in his own words, "beat his ass off."

Being meek and poor are not requisites for good works, I know. Quite the contrary. But it surprised me to find that this prominent civil rights leader was such an astute businessman, and, oddly, I was disappointed. "He's no saint," I blurted out to my attorney. "Charles Evers is interested in"—and I spat out the word as if it were an obscenity—*"money."*

My attorney laughed. "Well, now, isn't that as American as apple pie?"

My impressions of this remarkable man evolved over a period of time, starting with a brief encounter when I was a "black" woman working on my book, *Soul Sister*. It moved into a second stage when as black man and white woman we worked on his book in a Southern atmosphere of racial tensions and hangups and did daily battle with our egos and frustrations. In the end I came to see him as a medley of many impressions, a mixture of great strength and humility, by turns sad as the blues and ribald, complex, variable as the wind, yet essentially simple.

I can never forget my first meeting with Charles Evers. It was in 1968 and I was walking along Lynch street in Jackson,

Mississippi, with Alex Waites. He, along with a few other black leaders, including Aaron Henry, Vera Pigee and Cleo and Winson Hudson, knew I was white passing for black, and they helped protect me by taking me in as a visiting relative when I sought jobs as a black maid. Evers knew that I had lived with the Hudsons near Carthage, where there's a Choctaw Indian reservation; and he knew that because white men and Indians practice "nighttime integration" with black women it's hard always to sort out the colored mixture. He had heard how I'd confused one woman. "What are you?" she had asked suspiciously. "Choctaw?"

Now, on my last day as a black woman in Mississippi, Alex Waites and I were entering the NAACP offices when out bounded this large man with the face that has lighted up so many TV screens and the lives of so many black people. Before Waites could introduce us, however, Evers had his arms outstretched and I was quickly engulfed in a bearhug which for its warmth and generosity made me feel like a prodigal daughter come home. "You . . . you . . . you *Indian!*" he exclaimed. "Lucky you didn't get hired as a Choctaw. If there's anything these Kluxers treat worse than a nigger, it's an Indian."

Such chance meetings are usually impersonal, yet carry with them an uncommon clarity. The complexities of character later cloud such a first uncluttered impression, especially with a man of Evers' luminous personality.

In March 1969, after I had completed my book, my editor suggested a book on Charles Evers, preferably done in autobiographical form. I flew back to Mississippi, this time as a Southern white; and when Evers and I sat down to talk we were no longer soul brother and sister, warm, simple and trusting, but rather a black man and a white woman in a setting charged with taboos and myths. It was not our fault that the black man and the white woman in the South have never been free. It was not our fault that we still feel burdened by the centuries of lies the white man has bequeathed us. We sat down for a cup of coffee. But we knew that for more than 300 years the black man and the white woman could not look at each other, much less speak, and the circumstances were plainly not easy for either of us. He and I have both lived in the North, and had we met there we might have come to know each other in the Yankee way, which is cool, logical; but in Mississippi each of us reverted to type, which is to say, recovered our very Southern outlook and manners, putting each other through a labyrinth of nuances, one moment considerate and kind, the next hard and aggressive. Making a friend in the South always reminds me of Jacob's Biblical experience of wrestling with the devil, until he blesses him.

When I broached the idea of his writing a book, he just looked at me for a long interval. A man of moods, Evers can be sad one moment, his eyes revealing the burdens of centuries of grief, then suddenly he can flash a boyish grin that makes him look like a man without a care in the world.

He said finally, "I can't write no book." Then he added, "Since you're the writer, you can write the book—about me."

That wasn't what I had in mind, and I began to persuade him it ought to be *his* book in *his* words. "Writing is just having something to say," I argued. "The 'writers' of the Old Testament didn't write it out themselves. And Jesus Christ and Mohammed and Malcolm X all *spoke* their messages, and then others wrote their words."

Getting his verbal agreement was easy compared to getting him to sign a legal contract. Fiercely independent and not a little suspicious, he battled against lending the name "Charles Evers" to a binding document. "I don't sign contracts with nobody," he argued. Somehow, he conveniently lost the contract sent him by the editors in New York. It was many months later that he finally yielded and signed the paper.

Tape recorder in hand, I trailed Charles Evers with the persistence of a private eye. I listened to him speak to sophisticated, wealthy groups in the East and to "his" people in rural Mississippi, and in each instance he held his audience with a rough, natural magnetism. He had something to say, and he said it with candor and directness. He can be both vernacular and oracular. All the words in this book are his spoken words, recorded mostly on the run during history-making events: his race for and inauguration as Mayor, in voter-registration drives and during his days of bringing in new business ventures to the town of Fayette, which had not changed for the better since the days of Reconstruction.

As I trailed him, Evers shrouded himself in that mystique of leadership that marked the De Gaulles, Stalins, Churchills and LBJs of this world. There were times when I felt like a courtier or footman. He reminded me particularly of LBJ, for whom I had worked for three years at the White House. Each is a shrewd political creature, bigger than life, difficult if not impossible to capsule, pinpoint or characterize. Each likes to "keep his options open," even if it means unsettling everything and everybody in sight. I remembered that when LBJ took off in his presidential jet one never knew whether the journey was to see the Pope or his white-faced Herefords on the Pedernales. Similarly, I had no divining rod to predict Evers' plans. If I flew to Jackson, he was in Fayette, and if I arrived in Fayette, he might be in Jackson, New Orleans or the place I'd just left—Washington, D.C. Once I spent a week in a Jackson hotel waiting for him and when he finally came I exploded, "Listen, you make your living selling liquor and bread, but I make mine selling words."

A boyish grin with enough kilowatts to stave off an electrical shortage creased his face. I had said magical words: "selling" . . . "making a living." These, Charles Evers understands, and from then on our relationship became more harmonious and predictable. Evers works at moneymaking schemes, politics and rhetoric and civil rights all at the same time, and while he insists that business and civil rights don't mix ("You can't *eat* civil rights") the fact remains that for him they mix very well indeed.

When Evers was elected Mayor of Fayette he did not give up his home in Jackson. Instead he commutes between the two, maintaining a two-story brick house, with modest swimming pool, in the pleasant black Bellaire section of the capital but spending most of his time in a small apartment-office at his Medgar Evers Shopping Center in Fayette. The hub of the shopping center is a supermarket, small but modern and well-equipped. The center employs twenty persons, all of them residents of Jefferson County, of which Fayette is the county seat. Evers' wife Nan and four daughters often work as clerks and cashiers, but it is one of Evers' big disappointments that none of his daughters takes the business as seriously as he does. Probably no one else could. And this is because he alone knows the price he paid in facing down a Southern system that has insisted that "niggers" be kept in their place—that is, while a few might be show-pieces and make money singing or dancing or running for a touchdown, none were to compete against the white man as an entrepreneur.

Evers' life, with his pursuit of the dollar, contrasts sharply with the life of his martyred brother, Medgar, who has been termed "saintly" and "as gentle as a lamb." Supporters of Charles say he is driven by a desire to carry on the work of his slain brother, while critics say his interests are pecuniary. As I see it, both admirers and critics are right.

"Sometimes," Charles said, "people say, 'He's high on the hog,' and I say, 'Well, you go to hell. I worked fifteen and sixteen hours a day to get what I got. Sure I want to make money. That's why I'm in business, to make money. That's what my people need here—jobs, so they can make money. I don't see nothin' wrong with making money.' You can't do nothin' broke. If black people are to be really free in Mississippi, or any place else, we need to own something."

Charles says he went to Chicago to make money "and feed it back to Medgar, who didn't have nothin'." On June 12, 1963, Medgar Evers was shot in the back, fatally. And Byron de la Beckwith's fingerprints were on the suspected murder weapon. But the White Citizens Council, ably helped by the law firm of Governor Ross Barnett, got their man off. On the day that Medgar was murdered, Charles was back in Mississippi, and he vows he will not leave. He replaced his brother as NAACP field secretary until 1969, when he was elected Mayor of Fayette.

Evers' pride in his NAACP work flows from the progress he made on a wide front. At Medgar's death there were 28,000 blacks registered to vote, and the figure now is more than 250,000. All through the Sixties he participated in the boycotts of stores that would not hire black clerks and of the towns that would not hire black policemen or firemen.

No one who has seen Charles Evers can deny his courage. His walk, his words, his stance, his voice, convey absolute fearlessness. "The Lord knows," he says, "there's not a scary bone in my body." And even if there are scary bones, Evers simply acts as if fear is not present, which must be every bit as good as not having it in the first place. Throughout his early years of stealing, pandering and gambling (and he says, "Nobody had more houses of prostitution or dropped more policy than me"), he displayed physical courage. But he has gone beyond to a new, spiritual type of courage, which embraces an attempt to give a life of past error and hardship a new glory, a new meaning. In this respect he is no different from Tillich, John Donne, Genet and Malcolm X. Like Malcolm X, Evers is a master of what Professor Charles V. Hamilton has termed the "Politics of Spokesmanship," in which issues and leaders are projected forward as much through rhetoric and the mass media as through overt action. Evers' rhetoric has been used to politicize masses of people, and it is effective precisely because it is related to the culture, daily lives, values and aspirations of his people. Over and over again, Evers tells his people, "I'm no better than the least of you," and he is followed and admired because he is what they are, and trusted because he knows what the people need.

In many ways Evers is a man with a banner, running out front, shouting to the others, "Follow me!" He inspires confidence with his central message: "If I can get up off my knees and face the Man, so can you. If I can live without fear, so can you." Vicariously, through him, the blacks are touching their manhood, their womanhood. He is what an admiring Mississippi black has called "This Moses of Mississippi"—one to lead his people out of bondage.

Yet his voice reaches far beyond Mississippi. In one nationwide poll, Evers was voted one of the three black leaders Negroes trust and like most. He serves as national committeeman from Mississippi for the Democratic Party. He was offered the post of deputy chairman of the Democratic National Committee but turned it down. Then he was unanimously selected one of the twelve members on the Democratic National Executive Committee—and its first black member. "I guess it's an honor," Evers said, "a personal honor. But who in hell needs personal honors? We need some results." "Results," as he sees it, mean the changing of minds, if not hearts, of Mississippi whites. In this struggle, I know how quickly he can act.

Once I came out of a Jackson hotel, got into a taxi and while the cab was moving, gave the address of Evers' home—2554 Queens Road. The white driver eyed me through his rear view mirror. "You sure you got the right address?"

"Oh yes," I responded.

He radioed, "Isn't Queens Road out there in niggertown?" Told that it was, he drove to cab headquarters, where, visibly shaken, he ordered me out of his cab: "I ain't gonna drive you out there."

I looked at my skin. I was accustomed to harsh treatment by Mississippi whites when I had passed as a black. Now what was the trouble? After a Vietnam war veteran volunteered for the mission of driving a white woman to a black neighborhood, I mused that there would have been no difficulty had I been black.

I felt powerless to act against this senseless discrimination, but when I told the story to Evers he immediately called the cab company owner: "This is Charles Evers talkin' "—and I could sense the uneasiness on the other end of the line. Evers recounted my experience and, like a teacher reprimanding a child, told the owner he didn't want to hear of anything like that happening again. Hanging up, Evers grinned. "He don't want to boycott, he'll behave, you better betcha."

Seeing him operate in Mississippi, one realizes that he has few peers. He has no one to turn to if he has a problem calling for superior wisdom or strength. Once he could call or walk into the White House and visit with John F. Kennedy, and then after Medgar and John Kennedy were slain, "Bobby and I became like brothers." Now, to me, Charles Evers seems very much alone, and perhaps when one person assumes leadership others come to see him always surrounded by many people—but essentially, always very much alone.

[xi]

One day I was at home in Washington, D.C., and Evers called from a large government agency, asking me to drive him to the airport. I drove up at the close of a workday and literally thousands of civil service workers swarmed out of their warren-like cells. I thought of their built-in pensions and securities, and then I saw Evers, holding a clear plastic bag with an extra suit and looking very much alone. Seeing him in that mass of men I realized that the human trait that advances man is not a "social" trait at all but rather the conviction of the individual that he is born free and has an inherent right to an I-Thou relationship with the universe without paying undue tribute to the opinions of society.

He got in my car and we were both silent as I steered through the traffic. "You got an extra five minutes?" he asked. After I nodded he directed me to Medgar's graveside in Arlington Cemetery. "I always try to get by here," he said.

We paused briefly, in silence, then drove on. The car radio reported yet another incident of white police shooting a black person, and I said, "No wonder blacks hate—" but he quickly cut me off: "No, Grace, *no*," and he said again what he has said so many times, that blacks weren't going to let whites teach them to hate. "No sir, we can't go that route."

When Medgar was shot, Charles said, "Sure, I thought of killin', but what could I do? I could kill ten of them. And then what?" And he continued, "Sure, I hate. I think I really do hate. But I hate so bad till I'm gonna make damn sure that I kill off all the cause that makes me hate."

Then he left to go back to Mississippi, where he admits that his "life's not worth a plugged nickel," because a racist can shoot him just as one shot Medgar. Charles says he does not fear that, because he wants to go the way Medgar did, trying to make his life count for something.

Grace Halsell
Washington, D.C.
February 1971

[xii]

1

Fayette, Mississippi, 1971

Now that I've been elected Mayor of Fayette, Mississippi,
I don't want anybody to think for one minute that I'm
a saint. I ain't nobody's saint. But I am a man. I don't
want to be remembered as a politician. I want to be known
as a man who cared enough to tell it all about his life,
the bad and mediocre parts along with the good. Whatever I've done, I'm man enough to admit it. I'm not going
to lie about it for anything. I don't have to.

Today I'm nothing I used to be. I've left that part of
the world. But it's worth telling so young blacks will know
that what's important is not what you were yesterday, but
what you are today that counts. But I always go back to
my past. I'm fighting the past. Maybe there's no end to it.

Whatever I am today is because my brother gave his life.
I happen to have come in and taken up where Medgar left
off. And I don't take any credit. Anybody could be where

I am if they wanted to pay that price. Maybe he's living on in me in a way. I know I'm living on in him. Nothing could make me return to my old life now.

The first thing is I'm a loner. I wonder sometimes if I trust anybody at all. From banks on out I don't trust things or people. One thing I remember about my friend Bobby Kennedy was I trusted him; I knew he'd never lie to me. And he trusted me. Not trusting can make you lonely. And I'm a lonely man, I guess, because that's what I want to be. I drive up on the red mud tracks on my land overlooking the lake I've just bulldozed and look out over the blue hills and the gray skies and the moss dripping from the bare gum and magnolia trees and just wait there for several minutes to make all the decisions I have to make. Nobody is going to help me with those decisions. Nobody could.

My wife Nan. Oh Lord before I go any further let's not forget Nan who's always there when I need her, loyal, kind, never asking me what I'm up to or why this or how come that or telling me do the other but just sticking by me. Not a man in the world doesn't need somebody warm when the world's caved in on him. Nan is that somebody for me. And I haven't been all that good to her by a far cry.

You see, I'm a reformed hustler. I'm a reformed, tough nightclub operator. I've been in policy and bootlegged whisky and once had three women pregnant at the same time. And I'm not as poor as I was twenty years ago, which was damn dirt poor.

I know I haven't always been an angel. I've created a lot of ill will among people just trying to get ahead. But that's what it's all about. Men have come at me with knives, and I've had to cut them down. And I've cut others down politically and still others down economically. You've got

[2]

to be sure of folks. Like when someone says, "I don't like that bastard Charles but at least you can trust him." Or when people say to me, "I hate you but at least I've got to say you're fair." To me that means everything.

My wife was a little upset about something somebody wrote about Martin King. Well, Martin was a man and he enjoyed life. So what? If he had his eye on another woman, so what? Show me a man that doesn't have another woman. Show me a woman that doesn't have another man. My position is: You've got to tell it yourself. Then nobody can tell a thing on you. Yes, I've had whorehouses. Yes, I ran policy wheels, I dropped policy, I picked up policy. Sure I've gone with black women, white women. Sure I've had a few babies. So who hasn't had babies? Those who haven't had babies just didn't let them get here. I'm going to let mine get here, and I'm going to take care of every one of my babies. Can't any of my women who had babies by me say I didn't take care of them.

Can't anybody blackmail me. Can't tell more on me than I've already told. Show me a man who hasn't made a mistake. Show me a man who's not still making them. But the big part is, be big enough to admit it. Show me a man who hasn't slept with a woman that wasn't his wife. Or a woman who hasn't slept with a man that wasn't her husband. But I've never mistreated my family, never denied them anything. And I don't allow anybody to mistreat them. If I had another woman, she'd better not show any disrespect toward my wife and children. She'd better not. And if you saw me go to a motel room with a woman, so I went to a motel room with a woman. The only thing you could do is tell my wife, and I'd say, "Well, honey, listen, it's your choice. If I'm guilty, I'm guilty. You don't have to stay here, and if you go, I'll take care of you for the rest of your life. But if you're going to let someone run you away from me because someone said they saw me going to a motel room with a woman—then you have to go."

I tell all of this because in this country a man who gets elected to public office—especially a black man—can't be a "paperback," something that's going to crush if you touch it. You've got to be tough enough to go out and take them on. You've got to throw them off, and you got to keep going. You've got to be independent.

As Mayor of Fayette I make just $75 a month, and I turn that money back. So, I earn my living from the Medgar Evers Shopping Center; and in 1970 I opened a nine-unit motel with an air-conditioned restaurant and a lounge with carpet on the floor. No more dusty rat-and-roach place. It's called the Evers Motel, Restaurant and Lounge. The motel was once owned by whites, and it was a racist place, like everything else around here. So I bought the thing and changed it. That's what money can do—it can change a racist place into a non-racist place. Someone asked, "Are you going to let whites stay at your motel?" I said, "Yes. You got to remember that the only color that's important to me is green."

Sure it's a moneymaker. But it's also a service. If whites can have businesses, blacks can have them. All you have to do is save your money. I don't drink, I don't smoke, I don't gamble, I don't dip, I don't chew. So I take my money and invest it where people can see it. I built a big lake. It looks like a lot of money, but it was just a matter of getting a couple of bulldozers in there pushing dirt and banking it up, at $18 an hour for about a week, and you've spent $1,000 and it looks like you spent $20,000. With two bulldozers working for a week, you can turn an awful lot of dirt. I have a thing for lakes. Probably because white folks never let us use lakes. It's kind of a symbol for black people today.

[4]

You can't be as sassy as I am and be broke. If you're poor, someone is going to say, "Well, you owe this note." That's why I try not to go into debt. Can't anybody in this country say to me, "All right, we're going to foreclose."

Everything I have I worked for. The kind of work might not be the kind that will go down in a good-deeds book, but I worked for it. You never see where I held up anybody. I took money in policy, but they were trying to win some money and I was trying to win some. But that was many years ago, in Chicago, and I'm not doing those things now. It's not what a man *says* but what he really is that counts. I can say a whole lot of things but I know what I really am—and that's important. I think that's what made Medgar and me so close. We didn't lie to each other. And the same with all the people I've associated with. If I told them I'd do a certain thing, I'd do it.

Being Mayor of Fayette has been difficult, but I've enjoyed every minute of it. The mere fact that I'm still alive is the greatest thing of all. Fayette is the only town in Jefferson County, but we serve the whole county, which is 10,000 people. The town corporation limit only consists of about 1,700. Fayette is 70 percent black. And I knew that all I had to do was to get my folks to believe in me and get them to understand that they're as great as anybody else, that they have no tails, and that they don't have to walk around feeling inferior.

You've got to realize that Fayette was one of the worst towns for blacks in Mississippi. There was so much fear there you could see it in the eyes of the black folks. Just a few years ago blacks couldn't walk in the street with a white shirt on unless they were a preacher or teacher. There wasn't a single black registered in Fayette or the entire county in 1964. Sixty percent were on welfare and most of the rest were unemployed. Blacks got half as much schooling as the whites, and the whites were ignorant.

They had two or three old policemen there that didn't even finish the third grade, could barely read and write, and their one job was to *keep the niggers in their place.*

Our people are beginning to have some dignity, some pride. You've never seen a community with the kind of pride the black folks have in Fayette. My proudest accomplishment is that they believe in me, that they trust and follow me. You can't buy that.

In Fayette we are getting our young people involved. I know they won't make the mistakes that I made. They won't have to do the kind of hustling I did. They're going to be a part of the community, a part of the government, and they're going to make our state the greatest state in the nation. They're going to make Mississippi just as good as it has been bad. Blacks have never had a mayor they could go to, so they bring everything to us now.

Being the Mayor of a small town, you're also the judge and the prosecuting attorney. So whenever a husband and wife have a little spat the wife will get angry and make out a warrant for his arrest and we serve it and arrest him. But twenty minutes later his wife says, "Mr. Mayor, would you let him go? He didn't mean it."

We've had problems, plenty of them. To begin with certain people in the last administration went on a spending spree just before they left office. I'm not blaming the former mayor because I don't think he knew what was happening. And I've got to point out that he and some of his people said they'd help us out wherever they could when they left, and they have. But when I took over there wasn't money to pay salaries or run the damned town. I had to go out and beg.

I don't have any pride. I'm going to beg everybody for everything I need to help my people. Like somebody said, "Every time you look up, you see Evers beggin' on TV."

That's right. We've got nothing. Nobody going to give us anything if they don't know about us.

I went on the Walter Cronkite show and each viewer was asked to send in $1. In ten days we had collected over $100,000. Other radio and TV shows got us money, too. I think listeners to the Martha Deane Show on WOR in New York sent close to $30,000. Detroit Catholics sent in a flood of one-dollar bills that totaled near $30,000, after *The Detroit Catholic* printed an appeal under the heading: "Dr. King's Dream Worth a Dollar?" The biggest single private cash donation we got came from an anonymous Mississippi donor: $1000.

Some folks said, "How do we know you're going to spend all that money right?" And I said, "You don't know. But trust us. Give us a chance, and see if we don't build a community."

And we have. With the money we were able to employ eight persons at city hall, where there used to be just one. We have an economic-development team, a city clerk, an accountant, a secretary and a bookkeeper, too, so we don't make a mistake and overspend.

We also got a Ford Foundation grant of $500,000. We appreciate the $131,000 health-planning grant we got from Washington. But I didn't bow or scratch to get it. I've sent in a number of proposals, which they've been free to accept or reject as they like. The health-planning grant will make it possible for us to start building a new medical center, which will be named for Medgar. We've now got three full-time local doctors for Jefferson County's 10,000 people (instead of the one we formerly had), and Michigan specialists come down in pairs for two-week stays on a rotation basis. And the drug companies have given us about all the medicines we need. They've been beautiful.

When I visited Philadelphia, Pennsylvania, recently the

Police Chief and some of his detectives got together and bought us a new Oldsmobile police car. In New York, the same thing. The police there collected enough to give me a Ford, so I wouldn't have to go round in that old pickup I used to drive. And a good friend who asked to keep his name a secret donated a fully equipped, air-conditioned ambulance to Fayette. The people who did these good things were white and black, and I'm not about to forget it.

In the little more than a year since we've begun to manage our own affairs here in Fayette, the whole town has changed. And I'm talking about for black folks *and* white folks. Instead of hopeless expressions you'd see on everybody, why now they're perky. Most of the young people didn't finish high school. You bet they're going to finish now.

No more women making $4 or $5 or $10 a week for six or seven days' work, no sir. I don't know of a single woman now who makes less than $30. The woman's biggest friend was the boycott. We tried it first in Natchez. Just pointed out to people how they were being robbed. Nobody believed a black man could walk the streets of Natchez and tell white folks they were wrong. Fifteen hundred of us did, though. We just got up on the sidewalks and told people how wrong and mean they had been and that we weren't going to take it. This kind of thing gave the black folks there some guts.

And we didn't use violence either. We used the old spiritual method. You ought to come down and see how we do. We have our own choirs, our own soloists, our own preachers.

I always say God will deliver us—but we've got to help him. Got to register. Got to own something. We took nickels and dimes and made our own cooperatives: liquor stores, groceries, clothing stores. We stopped shopping where they wouldn't hire blacks and pay them at least $30 a week. They came around.

Sometimes we had to discipline our own people, just like Momma did with us. Tan them a little bit. Nothing wrong with disciplining your own family. I'm not saying we beat anybody up. We took care of them in a way they understood. People would catch them coming out of an uncooperative store and take their bags away from them, destroy the bags. Why they were paying to keep us in slavery. Or a motor would lock on a car. There might be a bit of sugar in the gas tank. Then occasionally maybe somebody . . . I didn't do it . . . but somebody would send a brickbat through a window around midnight with a telegram saying "You shopped at such-and-such-a-place."

See, people don't always obey because they want to. They usually obey because they *have* to. And they have to stop spending their money in racist-bigot-hater stores.

My main goal is to kill welfare in Jefferson County. But since most of my people there had little or no schooling and didn't know how to work at any kind of job, we opened a new Vocational Training school, where men are taught woodwork, brick-masonry, concrete work and how to be electricians and welders. And we got a Manpower Training school, which is more technical. Then the next thing I had to do was to get out and bring in some jobs. You got to remember that we had nothing. Thank God we now have several plants under construction: Thompson Industries, a subsidiary of International Telephone and Telegraph Corporation, will make electrical wiring for automobiles and will employ 150 people; and we have the Commercial Chemical company, which will build a half-million-dolar plant; then there's a concrete-manufacturing company that will make concrete for home building. We received a new garbage truck and a mechanical ditch-digger and a billing machine. Before, they wrote out all

[9]

the bills by hand. And we got a swimming pool that we didn't have before. The white children are welcome there, but if they don't want to come, they're welcome to stay out and sweat, too.

The whites have bucked us every chance. Like, the county officials forced us to move a six-foot granite monument to Medgar from a county-owned park to the city-hall grounds across the street. Then we put up WELCOME TO FAYETTE signs showing a black hand shaking a white hand and the State Highway Department made us take them down. We got them up again, though.

We don't allow harassing of anybody in Fayette any more. A policeman who shoved anybody around in Fayette would get fired on the spot. I don't know of another Mississippi mayor who'd fire a policeman for mistreating a black man.

Policemen sometimes think that because they have a gun they can do their thing. One of our policemen wrote out a ticket on a white driver. *"Doing 25 miles an hour in a 45 mile speed zone."* Just like that. The court was just jammed. You've never seen the kind of court I have. Nowhere. Just plain talk, common sense, that's all.

I told the officer: "You have this young man here charged with doing 25 miles in a 45-mile zone. Is he guilty or not guilty?"

"I meant to write 45 in a 25 zone!"

"Now, officer, you said he was doing 25 in a 45."

"But he was . . . I mean I put it in the wrong place . . ."

"If you're no better an officer than that . . . drag a man into court . . . write a ticket saying he's doing 25 in a 45-mile speed zone, then you have to go back to school some more. I will apologize to this young man for your lack of concern. I want him to know it. He's got nothing to worry about. You're supposed to preserve and protect, not to forget or harass. Do you understand that, officer. You have no comment. Just say Yes.

"Now, you, on the other hand, young man. If you come speeding through this town, doing 45 in a 25, you're going to pay for it. I know you were speeding. But he didn't write it right. The officer didn't perform his duty right. And you're going to go free, so get out of here."

I think the whole future of Mississippi depends on what we do in Fayette, because it is the only biracial town in Mississippi that's governed by black people. Unless we prove beyond any doubt that blacks can run the kind of town that America was built for, it's going to be detrimental to black people all over this country because they are going to be judged by what we do in Mississippi. That's why we're being very careful about the kind of administration we run. We can't afford to have the kind of conduct that's seen in most every other town. We can't have prostitution and gambling houses. We can't tolerate the numbers game. And I tell my black brothers, "Let's take our town and our county politically and then share it with our white brothers—even though they never did it with us." And we have. Ten of the 26 people on the town payroll are white.

And I'll go further: I'd like to do as governor what I've done as mayor. I could do for the state what I've done for Fayette: bring in industry, give people jobs, stop all this talk of hate. And I believe that I could help stop Mississippians from hating one another. You couldn't isolate me from the people.

You don't think that after all I've been through I could ever think of myself as "above" or separate from the people. Some politicians isolate themselves because they want to be isolated. No security men could isolate me. If I'm going to go, I'm going to go. And I'd rather go while I was out working than while I was hid behind some secret-service man.

President Nixon said when he took office that he wanted to bring us all together. But he picked a vice president who's split us apart. What you need are men in power who will talk about togetherness after the election as well as before. And who think togetherness in their souls. That's what'll bring us together.

And I think the administration realizes how wrong it's been and is going to change. Maybe for political reasons, but I couldn't care less why. Let's be fair about the Nixon Administration. It's done more to integrate schools in my state than any administration we've ever had. So many things they *didn't* do. But *that* they *did* do. Man, Nixon's really cracked down. There's not a school in this state that some blacks are not in.

People at the top are important to the attitudes of the folks below them. What I say in Fayette has a great deal to do with how people act. If there's one thing I've learned it's that most social problems come from elected officials. The beatings by policemen, the beatings by deputy sheriffs, all the ugly things have been permitted my mayors and sheriffs. Now that blacks control Fayette, it would be simple to start unloading hate, start talking about "getting those honkeys," or ordering my policemen to begin collaring "crackers" and "peckerwoods" and fine them $200 every time they turn around. But this town would be a nightmare. Whites and blacks would be jumping all over each other. We can't afford that. What I'm telling you is that the men who sit at the top have to set the example to bring our communities together.

Really, the threats are getting worse. When I was doing NAACP field work in the Sixties, occasionally a Kluxer would threaten me, like: "Nigger, we're gonna kill you like we killed your damned brother." But now that I'm

[1 2]

Mayor the threats don't let up. People call me on the phone, and some even tell me their names. I can't figure it all out.

Strangest of all, most of my hate mail comes from New Jersey and Florida. But I'm in Mississippi. If I were holding some national office, I'd understand better. I'm not bothering anybody in New Jersey. Maybe it's just some Mississippi folks who've gone north or to Florida.

It would be nice to do without bodyguards. But it would be foolish, too. So I have a few of them when I talk to large groups of people. A bodyguard can't really save you, I suppose, but he can sometimes detour a kook with a gun. But then again, look how they did Bobby Kennedy. Not more than two feet from him. And his assassin knew all about Bobby's bodyguards.

I think about dying quite a bit now. Why should they leave me around? I'm saying the same things that Martin, Medgar and Bobby said. They don't want us around. And usually if they can't find a white nut to do their killing, they'll hire some poor black.

Well, a man has to keep on. There'll be more assassinations, sure as hell. Blacks and whites alike are going to catch some bullets down here. I'll probably catch one myself one of these days. After all, down South a man who says niggers are just as fine as white folks has signed his own death warrant. That's why I intend to enjoy every moment of the life I have. Life is too short anyway. Lot of folks keep waiting on tomorrow and tomorrow and tomorrow. I'm living for today, doing the good I can right now. I'll worry about dying when I'm gone.

2

I knew both John and Bobby Kennedy, but Bobby much better than John. Bobby and I got very close. He was a man I loved like a brother. I had faith in him because he always said what he meant and meant what he said.

Right after Medgar's death, the President asked me to come to the White House. We were alone in his office. Mostly we just talked about Medgar. I remember him saying these words: "I will do anything I can to keep something like this from happening again. We can't let your brother die in vain. This has to end. I just hope his death will not be any deterrent for your struggle to be free. I hope no one will be cowed by this. I just want you to know that any time you need me, all you have to do is call."

After that, I stopped by the White House several times. Never needed an appointment or anything. Never. The

Kennedys couldn't have been kinder or more considerate. I met Jacqueline Kennedy several times, but I can't say I know her. And I don't really know Joan either. The one I knew well was Bobby. And Ethel, of course.

Bobby called me constantly after Medgar was killed. About once a week at least. When his brother met the same fate as Medgar, first thing I did was get on the phone and call him and say I'd be there.

Thereafter, when we did get together, we'd cuss and fuss and raise hell with each other. Bobby was a little slow on civil rights. Didn't move fast enough for me. I'd tell him to hire some blacks for his office. Once he said to me, a little bit miffed at all the harassing I'd given him, "Charles, what *do* you need?" It didn't take me long to answer. A short while I'd been leading a demonstration on Capitol Street in Jackson, and one of those damned old U. S. Marshals shoved me off the steps. I said, "Bobby, we need a good U. S. Marshal for Jackson." He said, "Well, get me one and he's yours." Just like that. This was when he was still Attorney General under President Johnson. Well, I went and got him one right away, and he's still in Jackson. First and only black we ever had.

When Bobby decided to step down as Attorney General I went to him and begged him not to leave. He told me something I've always remembered since then. "When they scream and holler for you the most, Charles, that's the time to get out. If you stay on till you're not wanted, then they scream you down and that's worse. Right now, when I know people want me, I can move on to something else." It didn't make sense to me then, but now I know what he was talking about.

One day he said, "I'm going to run for the Senate from New York. Will you help me?" Did I campaign for him? You bet. We went everywhere together. I've got pictures of us both getting off the *Caroline* in Buffalo, Syracuse,

Rochester, all over. He couldn't read a speech worth a damn. I recognized this failing in him because I can't do it myself. I used to tell him, "Now Bobby, don't read it this time. Just talk." But I'm even worse then he was.

When we were on the road, I always used to tell him, "Bobby, you just take care of the white folks. Leave us colored folks alone. I'll tend to us." Afterwards, when he was running for President, he said to me, "O.K. now Charles, I'm going to take care of the white folks. You take care of the colored folks and the Jewish people."

I'll never forget that Senatorial campaign, though. The NAACP brass was against him then, because they wanted to see Senator Keating keep his seat. He'd voted right. Up and down the line. They told me I had to work with Keating. I said, "I don't give a damn what he's done. He's no Bobby Kennedy. Bobby's my man."

At the New York State NAACP convention in 1964, they invited Keating and not Bobby. I was the guest speaker. All of Keating's henchmen were there, tearing Bobby into little pieces. I almost cried. Poor Bobby didn't have anybody there to defend him. I got a lot of notes, warning me off. One said: "Charles, we know Bobby's your man. But not *here.*" That was from one of the top NAACP boys. When Keating got up, he said Bobby'd turned his back on civil rights, that he'd run out on this and that.

I was the last speaker, and finally my time came. I was just fuming inside and out. I said, "I came to speak at the NAACP banquet. But I didn't know I was going to come here and sit in agony and take the kind of abuse I've heard here. Now it's my turn to speak, and I'm not going to speak about the NAACP. I'm going to speak about Bobby Kennedy. He has nobody here to defend him but me. I just want you to know, Senator Keating, that everything you've said here about him is not true. Bobby didn't leave office to run out on Negroes, but to do better for them. As Senator from New York. I've lived in New York. I want you to know here and now that when you invited me here, you invited Bobby. I want every Negro in this state, every Negro who believes in me, to go out and vote for Bobby for senator. Sure, Senator Keating, you voted right. But that's all you ever did. You can't show me one Negro on your staff anywhere. You can't show me a single bill you've introduced that's helped Negroes. Look at Harlem, look at Bedford-Stuyvesant, look at all the places Negroes live. What have you done there?"

Poor Senator Keating was sitting right there. I even was forced to leave the hotelroom I'd booked, and the NAACP threatened to fire me. I told them to keep their damn money (I was making under $10,000 a year from them then. Maybe it was closer to $6,000). But I also told them they were not taking over the NAACP in Mississippi, because Medgar, Aaron Henry and I had built it. From two branches to sixty-four. And, believe me, I never left that office.

While Johnson was still President, and before he decided not to run again, Bobby talked with me about running for the presidency, and I said, "Bobby, it's going to be hard for me to support you over Johnson. I'm going to be frank with you. President Johnson has done more to help the poor blacks and the poor whites than any man I know —including Abraham Lincoln. But now for you to come out against him is going to split the civil rights forces down the middle."

And he said, "Well, Charles, I know that, and I don't plan to run. But I'm being asked to run, and I'd like to talk with you about it."

I said, "Well, I would hate for you to do it. Because I couldn't come out against President Johnson."

When I first met Bobby, he was no different from everybody else. He wasn't a racist, but he just didn't know what was happening. He wasn't any saint. He was just like every other white man. He was selfish, he was conceited, he didn't feel that the black man and the poor people were his problem. But he began to learn. He found out how horrible it was to be a black man in this country, and he began to use his influence to do something about it. He began to feel his responsibility as a public servant. He went with me to the poverty areas in the Mississippi delta. Once he sat on some broken-down bed in a shack near Greenville and tears ran down his cheeks. "I'm going back to Washington and do something about this," he said.

Blacks loved Bobby Kennedy because of what he learned to be, the things he did. And I never begged him for a anything. Can't a Kennedy ever say he gave me a quarter. In any kind of way. I'm just as independent as they are. So it wasn't what he could do for me financially. It was because I believed in his philosophy. If he said it, you could put your foot on it. When I was going to run for lieutenant governor against Byron de la Beckwith (the same Beckwith whose fingerprint was found on the rifle that killed Medgar) in 1967, Bobby said right off, "No, Charles, you'll get in trouble if you do that. It's a spite thing with you. Don't waste your time. It's not worth it. You know you can do too much good otherwise." I took his advice.

I'll never forget when we were together at Dr. King's funeral. I just broke down. It seemed like I had lost almost everything. I had lost Medgar, we had lost John—and now Martin. I went all to pieces. Bobby and Ethel stayed with me and got me together. When we came out of the church we walked through a crowd of thousands, and they shouted, "Hey, there's Senator Kennedy!" We were in a funeral procession, not on some campaign trail, so I said to Bobby, "Look, why don't you stay in line and we'll walk straight on through." But Bobby was one of those hardheads, and I could tell he didn't like me telling him what to do. So Earl Graves, who was on his staff, got on one side of him and I got on the other. The people were pulling on Kennedy and Earl was trying to protect him. But Bobby said, "Get out of the way, Earl. If they want to shake my hand, I want to shake their hand." And he shoved Earl out of the way.

I said, "Earl, if he doesn't want us to protect him, let him go. Just let them snatch at him, and when they get through with him, he'll see."

Someone took Bobby's coat and took off. So there he was in his shirtsleeves. And I said, "All right, just keep on, just keep on."

And he said, "Aw, Charles, you don't have to rub it in."

"Just keep on. Can't tell you anything," I said. "These people will snatch your cufflinks and have the shirt off your body next time."

You could tell he knew he was wrong for getting out of the funeral procession, so he got back in line and we went on to the cemetery, where they had another service. And Bobby had to go on the platform with the other dignitaries in his shirtsleeves.

The night Bobby was shot we were all sitting around in a hotel suite in L.A., watching the returns come in. Rosy Grier, Rafer Johnson, Steve Smith and his staff, well, a group of us, and Bobby came and sat right in the middle of us. And my friend Chuck Quinn of NBC was there. CBS had projected Bobby as the winner, but Chuck Quinn wouldn't, so I said, "Chuck, what the hell! Why don't you go ahead and project him?"

"Well, no. We're going to make sure."

And I said, "I believe you're against Bobby."

"No-o-o."

"Yeah, I believe you are. I believe we have an anti-one-of-us up in here."

And Bobby said, "What about it, Chuck?"

And Chuck (just as serious) said, "Well, we're not quite ready yet, Senator."

Then the people downstairs in the ballroom chanted, "We want Kennedy! We want Kennedy!" We could see it in the room on the TV. Bobby made a point to thank those who had helped him, and he went around to each person, and I said, "Don't thank me. I'm doing what I'm doing because I believe in you." And then he asked everyone to be sure and come to the news conference right after his talk. Finally, Bobby said, "Okay, let's go." So they all got up and I just kept sitting there. Then he said, "Charles, are you going?"

And I said, "No, you don't need all your black boys with you. I'm going to stay behind and watch you from here."

And he said, "Aw, come on."

"Naw, I'm going to stay here and watch you from here."

"Okay."

But as he left, I could tell he wanted me to come, and something told me I had better get on down there. I gave him time to push through the crowd, then I went on down. Bobby was just standing up to speak. I pushed through the crowd and got right in front of him so he could see me—I wanted him to know I was there. I crooked one of my fingers—a sort of signal we had—and he nodded his head. But I remember the mikes wouldn't work, and Bobby said something like "What's wrong with these damned mikes?" But they finally got the mikes to working. And there were balloons all over the place.

Well, he made his speech and turned to go off the stage, and I turned to join him. I thought he had gone out the front door and up the elevator to the news conference. But instead he turned to go out through the kitchen. I didn't even know there was a kitchen back there at all. I guess I was about five feet from him, and I started pushing through the crowd of people, but it would've taken about five minutes to get even another foot. So I sort of waved my hand to him, and in a split second I heard that *phat-phat* sound, and I thought it was balloons, then the crowd just swirled together and someone screamed, "Oh, they shot the Senator!" Then I was just like in football. I pushed myself through the crowd, and when someone tried to block me I just knocked him down and got to Bobby's side. Ethel was screaming.

I don't know. It just doesn't make sense. I can hardly talk about it, even now, because he meant so much.

3

Decatur, Mississippi, 1922–30

My Momma was strong and my Daddy was strong, and
they influenced my life the most. I got my religion from
my Momma, and my Daddy taught me not to be afraid.
Daddy was a mean man. He couldn't read or write, but
he didn't back off of any man—white or black. His name
was Jim Evers, he was tall, over six feet, like me. He didn't
have the kind of trouble that many blacks had, because
Daddy was so mean. He'd just raise all kinds of problems.
He worked hard, but he wasn't a bit scary. He taught me
that most white folks are cowards. If they haven't got you
outnumbered, you can back 'em down. So I've always
thought I could outwit most white folks. Being black, you
gotta learn that, just to survive. The only thing I didn't
agree on with my Daddy was when he'd say. "That's a
white man's job." There's no such thing. But he still had
that belief that the white folks had indoctrinated all the

Negroes with: "All the good jobs are for white folks, and the hard, menial jobs are for black folks." And he believed that. I guess he did the best he could, though. I don't know how he lived through what he did, standing up to the white man as much as he did, because back in those days to kill a Negro wasn't nothing. It was like killing a chicken or killing a snake. The whites would say, "Niggers jest supposed to die, ain't no damn good anyway—so jest go on an' kill 'em."

My Daddy's father was Mike Evers. He wasn't a slave but a free man. He had 200 or 300 acres of land in Scott County, and he raised his own corn, potatoes and peanuts; he had peach trees, pecan trees, fig trees, and apple trees. He was independent, but it must have made the white folks very unhappy, because they took away that land from him, illegally. (And I'm going to look into that one of these days.) My Daddy's mother was named Mary, and she was part Creole Indian. She had long, straight hair and high cheekbones.

Most black people can go back only to their grandparents. No one kept records. We didn't have birth certificates. Each family had a big old Bible, and usually the momma would put in there when each of the children was born.

I don't really remember much about my grandparents. They all died when I was just a kid. And we don't have any long livers in our family. Most of our people die young. My father was a sawmill man, he stacked lumber. And he'd always follow those mills around. That's how we were over at Decatur, in Newton County, when I was born. Momma had been married before—and had children named Eva, Eddie and Gene. Then they had four more children. I was born in 1922, September 11th, then Medgar, Liz and Ruth. I was two years older than Medgar.

My Momma was a bright woman, and she wanted the

best things in life for her children. After I got elected Mayor of Fayette, I had one thought: *I wish Momma was here.*

She read the Bible a lot and had an understanding about it. She knew the time was coming when we were going to have to have an education. She just pounded it into our heads. She was shorty-short, about five-two, and when she was young she must have been a real doll, but later on in life she got stout. She had tiny feet, about a size four. She was part Indian and went barefoot most of the time. Her maiden name was Jessie Wright.

My great-grandfather on my Momma's side was half Indian. He was a slave, but from what I've heard he was one of the worst slaves they'd ever had. He'd just cause trouble and he just wouldn't take any abuse. His name was Wright—Medgar Wright. Medgar was named after him.

My Momma's father had a black mother and a white father. That's fairly common in the South, and that's why you see so many light-skinned Negroes. My half-sister Eva told me once about when she was just a kid and saw our grandfather for the first time. She was visiting at my Aunt Dora's in Forest, Miss. He came up to the front door and she ran to the kitchen. "Aunt Dora!" she said. "There's a white man at the door." My aunt laughed and said, "Eva, that's your grandfather." He looked just like any white man when you'd see him coming down the street. That's just how white he was. After 30 years up North, Eva's come back to Mississippi to help me run my restaurant. Eva's one sweet woman.

This half-white grandfather would stand up to any man, white or black, and he always carried a gun. Once a white man called my grandfather a "half-assed mulatto" and my grandfather shot at him. He didn't kill the man, but he had to leave town in a hurry.

Momma made all her clothes and all the clothes for my

[24]

sisters. She'd make them out of gingham cloth and old fertilizer sacks and flour sacks. We didn't know anything about silk panties and things like that. They had cotton drawers and petticoats.

Momma would make us pants. She'd buy blue denim and cut out pants and coveralls for Medgar and me—no pockets—and she'd be up all night sewing. She sometimes slept only two or three hours. I don't know how she arranged to get things done. But she's typical of the average black mother when it comes to working. I can just name you thousands of black women in those days who had to do the same thing. They'd get up about five in the morning, cook the breakfast for the husband and then go out and wash a big washing. They'd go to the field and chop cotton or plow, leave the field about eleven in the morning, walk all the way in from the field, sweaty and dirty, then cook dinner for the whole family, the white folks, too; and when they'd get through eating they'd have to wash the dishes up. Then they'd go back to the field about one-thirty or two o'clock, work till five or six. Then, in the evening, they'd have to milk the cows and feed the chickens before cooking supper.

Where they got all that strength? They had no choice. God's been good to us. He kept our black women strong and healthy.

We were all very close, our whole family was very close. But Medgar and I were together most of the time. You know girls are girls, what can they really do with boys? Just sort of be around and annoy them all the time. And our two sisters Ruth and Liz were very close. And Liz, she's not afraid of anything. She has her own grocery store now, in Chicago. So we all scratched together.

I may be even closer to Medgar now than when he was alive, if that's possible. He was the saint of our family and I cherished him. I didn't want him to leave Mississippi as

I had, because I knew how much he was needed here. So whenever he needed money, I'd send him down some.

Medgar never really knew how I earned my money in Chicago, and neither did Momma. I guess my Daddy sort of suspected. He could never figure out where I got all the money to pay their bills. He once asked me if I was bootlegging. I said, "Dad, you know I'd never bootleg." Of course, I was bootlegging, and right under his nose.

I was sort of fatherly with Medgar. Took care of him. We went to school together, always slept together. God, I remember us kicking each other out of the bed. But I always warmed it for him, because, man, was that bedroom cold, especially between those old sack sheets of ours. So I'd get a spot warm, then move over and let him have it because he was the baby. I remember putting my legs on him to keep him warm.

He was so clumsy. When we'd go fishing together I'd help him across the log bridge. But strong. We'd wrestle and box. Sometimes I'd let him take me, and sometimes he'd really take me. He was bookish, very sharp and very lovable. He never wanted to hurt anybody. All the battling and beating we got into, that was my doing, not his. I wasn't cruel or bitter, but I could be mean.

Momma used to say to me, "You're different. Medgar's sweet. But you're always in trouble." And Medgar used to say to me, "Charley, you're going to get into trouble." And I said, "I was born in trouble. Being a Negro, you're automatically in trouble."

As far as our girls went, Medgar and I had completely different types. On account of growing up in the Holiness Church, we never confided in each other about what we were doing to the girls. But I know he liked young, sweet, untouchable, frail little things who'd never give him anything. That is, they never became intimate with him. When he got a bit older, he became more aggressive.

I couldn't stand those young gals. For me, young gals are nothing but trouble. I liked older women who were able to do something for me. Young girls could do nothing but go to bed. I didn't need to go to bed. I needed protection. I was poor, had nothing. I wanted a woman who could at least buy me a shirt once in a while.

As boys, Medgar and I hated it when Momma or Daddy sent us into Decatur to a community store to buy flour or sugar. Soon as we'd go in the white men standing around there would start picking on us and trying to make us dance. "Dance, nigger!" The owner of the store was the worst of them all.

I used to swear to Medgar afterwards that some day I'd have a store and make white folks dance to my tune. Now I have a store, a couple of them, in fact, but I've never made anybody dance in them.

Usually, Daddy bought groceries on credit at the sawmill commissary. "Charge it," he'd say. Daddy would buy everything, even a box of snuff, on credit, and then every Friday or Saturday he'd pay. The store was run by a dirty white rascal named Jimmy Boware. This Jimmy knew that Daddy couldn't read or write, but Daddy was shrewd with figures. He could add and subtract and multiply in his head faster than you could with a pencil. And no one ever cheated him. One Saturday, Medgar and I went with Daddy to the commissary to pay his bill. I must have been about nine and Medgar about seven. When Daddy looked at the bill he told Jimmy Boware he'd overcharged him by $5 and something.

"Nigger," the white man shouted, "don't you tell me I'm tellin' a lie!"

Everybody knew how bad Jimmy Boware was. He beat Negroes, kicked Negroes, and this Saturday there must have been about ten or fifteen whites in the community store.

"Mr. Boware, you're just wrong," Daddy said. "I don't owe that much."

"You're callin' me a liar, nigger?"

Then Daddy said, "Well, I don't owe that, and I'm not going to pay it."

Jimmy stepped behind the counter to get a gun and Daddy grabbed a Coke bottle, broke it, pointed the jagged ends at him, and stood in his path. "If you move another step I'll bust your damn brains out."

Now there must have been about twenty whites who had gathered there. Medgar and I reached and got us a bottle each. Dad turned and said, "Get outside, boys," but we said, "No, Dad, we're not gonna leave you in here."

Boware said, "I'll kill you, you black sonofabitch!" and Daddy said, "You better not move. You better not go around that counter."

Daddy had nothing but a Coke bottle, but Boware was afraid to move, and we could see he was shaking like a leaf on a tree. Daddy kept his eye on him and backed us out of there. He'd bluffed every one of them, but when we were outside we thought they'd come after us and whip our daddy. We wanted to run, but Daddy said, "Don't run, don't run. They're nothing but a bunch of cowards."

We walked toward home, down along the railroad tracks, Medgar on one side of Daddy and me on the other. And we put our arms around him and he put his hands on our heads, and he told us, "Don't never let anybody beat you. Don't never let any white folks beat you." He said, "If anyone ever kicks you, you kick the hell out of him." It's because of my father that my nonviolence movement goes only so far.

White folks are always asking blacks, "When did you first realize you're black?" You know you're black from the day you're born. From the time your mother spits you out of her womb, you know you're different. We were born in our homes, in some old bed with some old woman midwife who pulls the baby from the mother's body. White boys and girls of my age were born in a nice clean hospital with sanitation. I was born in a house with flies.

The question "When did you know you were black?" is unfair. There is no black man in this country who'll tell the truth who won't say he has known he been black all his life. He has been mistreated like he's inhuman. I don't like to talk about it, because I get very upset—the way Momma had to wash and iron, and the way the children had to carry the clothes to the white man who'd send Momma a lousy 50¢ for her service. If a Negro tells you some little story about the moment he realized he's black, he's telling you a lie.

Being black is part of the air you breathe. Our mothers began telling us about being black from the day we were born. The white folks weren't any better than we were, Momma said, but they sure thought they were. When we'd ask why we couldn't do something or other, often she'd just say, "Because you're colored, son."

Our own people have been taught to believe that white is right and black is wrong. A lot of black parents would tell their children, "It's a white man's world, and you just happen to be here, nigger."

Medgar and I, right from the start, when we were little kids, were determined to prove that this wasn't a white man's world—or if it was, we'd at least get our share of whatever there was worth getting and see that some other black folks could, too.

Sometimes it was just no fun growing up black, like when we got it hammered into us to watch our step, to stay in our place, or get off the street when a white woman passed by so as not to brush up against her accidentally. To be black in this country is miserable more often than it's not.

We were brought up in the Church of God in Christ, also called the Holiness Church, and they don't believe in smoking, drinking, gambling, chewing, playing cards or dancing on Sundays. As a kid I was in church so much that I don't go often today. In fact I got so much church thrown at me then, I wonder if some of the wilder things I did later weren't just to fill up on things I was told to stay away from as a kid.

The deacon of my Momma's Holiness church was Will Loper, and I'd tell Medgar, "You're just like ol' Brother Loper," but Medgar resented this guy, because he was always up shouting, dancing, twisting and carrying on. Every Sunday, ol' man Loper would get happy and dance. Medgar'd get fighting mad when I'd call him Loper, and he'd take off after me, and I'd take off running. Then we'd be sitting around talking and I'd say, "You know, Lope—" and he'd look a snap right quick, and then sort of grin. The name just stuck, and I kept calling him Lope after we got bigger.

My Daddy was not as religious as my Momma. He'd go to her church, but he kept his own religion. He was Baptist. We used to have to go to church three times a week (all day Sunday). On Sunday morning it was Sunday school nine to eleven, and at eleven we'd get out about five or ten minutes and go right back in for church service. And we'd stay in there for the singing and praying and dancing till about one. Then the preacher would come on about one. He'd preach until about three. We'd get out about three or three-thirty, rush home and eat, and come right back at six o'clock for YPWW—the Young People's Willing Workers. We'd stay there until seven or seven-thirty and prayer service would begin at seven-thirty. And

we'd pray until about eight-thirty and then start the testimonials. That's when all the members got up and testified.
Can you imagine that! And after every testimonial we'd
sing a song.

Today all my civil rights meetings and business meetings
are very religious. If I run for governor the campaign will
be run the same way. Church became a part of me. And
we still sing those good ol' Christian songs. Anyway, after
the testimonials they'd take up collection. And then we
all go outdoors and up the street asking everybody to give
money to help pay the preacher. About nine-thirty or ten
the preacher comes in to the pulpit. You've been there
since nine that morning and about twelve hours later the
preacher is getting up again to preach the second time,
and he would preach *and* he would preach, and you'd get
home about twelve midnight, and you'd just *done had it*.
And a lot of times it'd be hot and you had to sweat and
fight those mosquitoes and try to go to sleep, and you
couldn't sleep, and the next morning you had to get up
and go to work or to school.

Tuesday night was prayer meeting. This would start
about seven-thirty and last a couple of hours. On Friday
nights you would have prayer meeting plus business meeting.

We had about three months out of a year going to
revivals. Medgar, me and all of us had to go to my
mother's church's revival—that lasted about two weeks—
and my Dad's church's revival, and some of the other
church's revivals. Preachers came from all over, and they
would preach and preach, and everybody was "saved."
This meant that we were "saved by grace," because we had
testified, and we were going to heaven and be with Jesus
when we died. We called those revivals our soul-saving
meetings. Every night you had to go and sit on that front
seat, and you'd better not talk. All Momma would do was

just look at you and you'd know, brother, she's gonna tear your fanny up. She wouldn't wait to get you home. Well, I don't object to that either. I'm proud my mother was like that because whatever we are, Momma and Daddy made us know right from wrong.

The big revivals, or tent meetings, opened with a picnic where everybody would bring their dinner and spread it all over tables, out in a pasture. People would come from miles around, and everybody seemed to be a kissing cousin. Everybody was getting saved and happy, they were shouting and they were kissing. Right now I kiss almost everybody I see. And it's because of my training. It's not that I'm being fresh. My Momma's people and all my people, everybody, we'd kiss each other when we saw each other. But a lot of people get the wrong impression of me, and I really wasn't aware of that until a couple of times women went a little too far about kissing. You know, they'd kiss back. So now I sort of lay my cheek against people's faces. But Momma always told us to kiss. She said, "It's showing that you care. It's affection that you show people, it's the concern." And when you're close to someone and kiss them on the cheek, it means you're not afraid of them. It means they're no different from you; and that we're all the same people. Caressing and comforting people is part of my life. That's what kissing means.

But I found that many people think I'm being fresh. And I'm only doing what Momma and Daddy, what all of us did. And most country people are that way, very affectionate. They hug you and kiss you. Aaron Henry and I, every time we meet, we hug. We embrace each other, and it's just a matter of being glad to see each other. Muhammed Ali and I once embraced right in the street. Because we hadn't seen each other in a long time; because we're friends and we're brothers—and that's the way it should be.

[32]

Besides going to church all the time we'd have prayers at home. We'd all get down on our knees and pray—every Sunday morning, and every night before we'd go to bed. In the prayers, Momma would say certain things out loud. She was talking to God, telling Him to help her take care of her children and help her sons to grow up to be men that the world would be proud of and not to be lazy rogues, haters or alcoholics. She'd just talk to Him, and we'd listen. And after we'd get through praying, my daddy would say, "You're goin' to church today, and after that you come on home. I don't want you gettin' into no trouble. But if anybody bothers you, you knock their ass off." So it was a combination of spiritual and natural teaching that we got.

Momma's old raggedy church leaked, so we didn't go when it was raining. Instead she'd read the Bible to us, and Daddy would always have something to do outside, and Medgar and me would say, "Daddy, Momma's gonna read the Bible," and he'd say, "Yo'll go on, listen to your Momma read the Bible. Get your Sunday school lesson," and he'd go out in the yard to take some snuff. Then he'd ease back in and we'd go up in his lap and he'd rock us to sleep.

On Sunday afternoons Daddy would tell us stories about when he was a boy, and we loved that. About how he used to steal watermelons and go swimming, buck naked, and how some white boys came and stole all their clothes, and how he and his friends had to make skirts out of pine branches to hide themselves. And Medgar and I'd sit there listening, wide-eyed, and we'd ask, "Did you, Daddy? Did you do all those things when you were a boy?"

I remember Daddy telling me a story about the evils of whiskey. As usual, he'd been drinking up a storm, raising sand, jumping onto tables and clearing them with his feet. Finally, he got to one table where there was "this little bitty old nigger," as Daddy called him. Couldn't have been much over five feet tall, probably weighed 130 pounds. My Daddy, remember, was big and mean and weighed over 200. Well, this little fellow said to him, "If you git up on that table I'll whup yo' big ol' ass." So Daddy jumped up on the table, kicked up his heels and began cussing him out. Without any warning at all, that "little nigger" just snatched the table out from under him and Daddy hit the floor with a plop.

"He beat me, he stomped me, he kicked me all over," Daddy said. "Then he snatched that half pint of whisky I had in my pocket and busted it clean over my head. Why that little bitty old nigger like to beat me to death." That really broke him up about drinking. Never did drink much after that, my Daddy didn't. Sure didn't walk on any more tables, for sure.

He told us all kinds of stories. About parching peanuts, roasting potatoes, and rabbit and 'possum hunting. Old folks never did give him a gun. "Y'ain' gwine have no gun, bo' . . . You'd shoot somebody." So old Daddy'd take out after the rabbits on foot. He'd find their sinkhole, wait there quiet-like, and send the dog on out after the rabbit. Sure enough, pretty soon the rabbit would come back and Daddy'd clobber him over the head with a stick. Said he used to catch enough in one day to last the year.

As Medgar and I grew older we became more sensitive about his taking all the money we earned. He'd hire us out to an old farmer. I made about $15 a month, which Daddy'd promptly snatch from me, and return maybe $2. His theory was, you don't need anything anyway, since I'm taking care of you and feeding you.

One day Medgar and I sat down with him and complained about handing over the money to him. "Listen," he said, "you think you can take care of yourself, you don't need to be in my house."

[34]

"Dad," I said, "It ain't *your* house. It's *our* house."

Whop! Bang! Daddy slammed me clean off the old bench we had, right onto the floor. Momma heard the racket and came in. She thought he was going to kill us. "Now Jim, honey . . ."

"Shut up, Jessie," he said. "Can't be but one Daddy in this house. When they get where they're telling me what to do, they better get out of this house."

Oh, we were smartass kids and Daddy knew just what to do with us. Seems we were always in the burial business. Medgar and I'd complain about the rickety old hearse we had. We called it the ambulance. And Daddy said to us: "Can you go buy 'nothern?"

"No."

"Then shut up talkin' 'bout this'n. Gotta' use what we got. Dead folks don't want to be toted away in this'n, let 'em find something better. Don't give a damn nohow."

We were the most comical family. Always had something going on in our house. Daddy used to chew Tuberose dip. When he'd come home, he'd make Momma a present of the coupon on the back. When she got 200 or 300 coupons, I think she could turn it in for an old dish. Every now and then Daddy's roll his old lip, swish around some dip and let fly on the floor of the house. Medgar and I'd wait a minute, then we'd jump up and one of us'd say, "Looky here, Daddy, right here on the floor. Somebody's spit on the floor." Shut yo' mouf' boy," he'd say, "know damn well who spit on that flo'." We never gave them a moment's peace.

Momma always cooked a big Sunday dinner, and some old rascal preacher would come eat with us. Medgar and I'd go out early Sunday to catch chickens and start ringing their necks, and Momma'd shout for us to ring 'em two at a time. Now, the average white person who kept chickens had nice chicken houses and kept the chickens away from where they were living, because a chicken is the filthiest thing you can get, but ours lived all around our shack and all we had to do was go out in the yard or on the porch to catch them. I'd ring one head off with my right hand and be killing another with my left hand, and those chickens would be gushing blood and flopping all over the place. Then Momma'd dump them in a tub of hot water and we'd all dive in to pick the feathers. Liz'd be shucking corn and Momma'd be frying chicken and baking good juicy sweet potato pie, or maybe pecan pie or blackberry pie or peach cobbler. We'd half-starve for the rest of the week, but that preacher had to have the best.

All the grownups sat down with the preacher, and he'd pray for about half an hour, then they'd dive in. The reverend liked Momma's white biscuits and her white gravy and her cornbread dressing, and he'd keep taking second helpings. And oh, he'd just eat and talk, eat and talk, eat and talk. And me and the rest of the kids would be outside sitting and waiting, and peeking in, watching them eat and just hoping they'd leave us some of the chicken.

One Sunday Medgar and I decided we'd get us some of the drumsticks and thighs, so I said, "Momma, come on out here, something going on out in the yard!" Then Medgar slipped into the kitchen to steal some parts, but clumsy as Medgar was, he dropped them on the floor.

"Reverend," Momma shouted, "come look what these mean boys are up to!" And the mean ol' preacher came running and got a long peach switch and whipped us all around the house, and Momma was chasing after us, too, and the reverend was telling Momma, "That's right, Miz Evers, you gotta break 'em for stealing. 'Cause if they steal chickens they'll be goin' downtown and stealin'."

Momma tithed as best she could, which wasn't much. Maybe she'd give 50¢ or a dollar a month to her church.

[36]

And she tried to teach us to tithe. I don't give 10 percent of my earnings right to a pastor, but maybe I pay someone's light bill or water bill, and maybe if someone dies and the family can't bury them, I bury them. Or someone gets stranded and needs help, I help them. Or some wino gets in trouble, I use a little money to help him. I always figure this is the way to help—without any thought of repayment.

Today I know a lot of young people resent the church because it's always promising heaven in the sweet bye and bye and lulling black people into accepting a subhuman way of life here on earth. But Momma was a different kind of religious person. She wasn't the kind who just believed in praying and sitting down. She taught us: "You pray—then you get up and go after it." She believed in prayer, and I guess I really believe in prayer, too. Because it does something to you. It may be all in your mind, but certainly it does something. Every time I get in a tight fix, I go off just for a minute. If I can pray just for a minute I'll be all right and can come out and meet it all head-on.

And I still say the Lord is up there and He hears you—if you believe in Him. You just got to believe in Him. It's like anything else, if you *believe* in something or other, that's what it's going to be. And before I make any speech I always ask the Lord to help me. "Now, You know I don't know what to say," I say. "You just tell me what to say and I'll say it." She always believed that prayer would get you through anything if you'd do your part. And I do, too.

Every spring and summer, Medgar and I and all the children were in our bare feet. We'd get briars stuck in our feet and we'd have to sit down and pull them off. Once every two years in the fall, Daddy used to carry us to town to buy us shoes. We'd get two pairs of shoes every two years. He'd buy us a pair of Sunday shoes—we called them our "slippers." We'd wear them to church and to funerals. And they'd always get them big enough for growth; if we wore size eight they'd get us ten so we could wear them two years. The minute you got out of church you pulled those slippers off and you went in your bare feet.

In the wintertime we had heavy, lace-up brogans for everyday wear. We had to put our brogans on when we got in from church in the wintertime. If Daddy caught us playing in our Sunday shoes he'd whip us good. "You'd better not be scuffin' in them Sunday shoes, son," he'd warn. And then just for the hell of it we'd go and do something in them—run around in the pasture and chase the cows out and get manure on our slippers. Then Daddy would beat the tar out of us.

We'd have to go pull off our Sunday clothes, too. We had one pair of green tweed pants for Sunday, and we'd pull them off as soon as we came back from church or come from a funeral. We'd put on coveralls, Medgar and me; or an old pair of blue jeans. And blue jeans, even to this day, remind me of how poor we were. It's a personal thing now. I just can't put blue jeans on to save my life.

But we were always clean. I remember Daddy wore coveralls all the time. And Momma could iron them better than anybody. Still, no matter how hard Momma worked and how much she prayed, we had a rough time. It's been no flowerbed for us, never was. No white person would take for one hour what most black people take all their lives. We didn't really go hungry, but we hardly had a change of clothes. I know this is why my half-sister Eva ran off and got married when she was sixteen. Marriage to her was having a pair of pretty new shoes.

At church the preacher was always talking about how "We're all God's children" and "No man is different from anybody else," so I'd ask Daddy, *"Why* are we different? The preacher don't say we *gotta* be different."

And he'd say, "Well, son, that's the way it is. I don't know what we can do about it. There ain't nothin' we can do about it. Because if we do anything about it, they kill you."

4

Decatur, 1930–33

Our next-door neighbor in Decatur was Mrs. Ada Atkins.
She was still bright as a lamp when she was eighty. She
started me off to school, in the first grade. But when we
were kids she'd watch out for us and whip us when we'd
get into devilment. Then she would tell Momma on us,
and Momma would whip us and Daddy would whip us.
On account of Mrs. Atkins, we'd have three whippings for
each offense.

Mrs. Atkins always had faith in us. She'd whip us in
and out of school, but she'd always say, "Them Evers boys
will be something one of these days." She only had an
eighth-grade education, but she taught us to believe in ourselves. She'd say, "You gotta stop being so high-strung, you
gotta start listenin' and not be so quick to get mad." And
then she'd add, "But you got it. You got the gumption."

Momma worked for a couple of white families near us,

but mostly for Mrs. Frances Gaines, who lived a mile down the road. For less than $5 a week, she cooked for them, washed, cleaned house, and took care of their kids, Bob and Margaret. We were real friendly with their kids, and to this day I still keep in touch with Margaret.

The Gaineses were not the most cheerful folks in the world, but they were always cordial to us.

Let me tell you something. Most of those white families treated their maids better than you'd expect. They had little choice. Even way back, black women have had more freedom than white women in the South. We always used to say the only people in Mississippi who have freedom are the white man and the black woman. The white woman and the black man had no freedom.

Women who worked as domestics at least had freedom of speech and freedom of complaint. They ran those households. They were indispensable. And many of them were pretty bold in their demands for the best money they could get and better treatment.

I ought to mention, too, that another of Momma's white employers, Mr. Jim Tims, who was the postmaster in Decatur, gave Medgar a letter of recommendation when he applied for entrance into Ole Miss. And that took some courage.

Momma and Daddy were very close, even though Daddy was tightfisted with the family and had his occasional fling with a girlfriend. But he always came home at night. Always. And as soon as he'd poke his nose in the front door, he'd start looking for Momma. "Where's Grimm?" he'd say. That was Momma's first husband's last name, and till the day he died Daddy called her by it.

She was proud of Daddy, and never gave him any backtalk. Daddy used to point out that her religion didn't permit it. But at night we used to hear them talking over things in bed. They'd talk on and on into the night. They loved and enjoyed each other.

A mother is closer to you than anyone else can be. It's hard to explain. We kids used to pester Daddy's girlfriends every time we saw them. Eva, especially, would fuss with them.

Momma never uttered a word about Daddy, though. She'd say, "We're just going to pray for him. Some day he'll change. And Charles, don't you go round trying to hurt women." But I always tried to get even with women for Momma's sake, and to this day I have a hard time liking most of them.

Momma would leave home early in the morning to go fix the Gainses' breakfast, and we'd have to stay home and eat cold cornbread and pot liquor or whatever was left over from supper the night before. While we'd be slopping the hogs or washing our clothes, Momma'd be down helping "Miss Ann" get her white children ready to go to school. Among us blacks, all white women were called "Miss Ann." All white men were called "Mr. Charley". Momma didn't have time to comb our sisters' hair and to get them ready, but she had to go and get the little white girls and boys ready and put them on a big shiny school bus. Medgar and I and the rest of us young black boys, we'd be walking to school in our patched-up blue jeans. These same little kids who'd been taught hate so long would ride along on this great big shiny yellow and black bus, and as the driver'd get close to us, where we were walking with no shoes on, he'd slow up and some white kids would spit out the bus on us and throw rocks on us. We'd have to jump in the ditch and dirty up our clothes and go on to school that way.

I'm all for busing today, by the way. I'm for *any* means to correct racial imbalance. If it means busing kids down from Decatur to Fayette every day, then let's do that. Once these kids go to school together, get to know each other, grow up together, they're going to be parents, governors, senators, congressmen, mayors, chiefs of police. They'll respect black folks when they get to know them, and that's the only way.

We'd go to school from the middle of October to the middle of February, and then the white folks would close the school down so all the young blacks would be able to join the old blacks and be available to work in their fields, cleaning and plowing and breaking the ground for the spring planting. We'd go to school only when the white folks didn't need us. That was four months of the year. Can you imagine! And that's why I don't pay any attention to this talk about being qualified. They never gave us a chance to qualify.

Most of the obstruction we meet comes under the heading of *"You're not qualified."* If they're looking for test pilots, no, I'm not qualified to fly a plane. So I don't ask to get up and fly the plane. That would be foolish. But I argue that if you need test pilots, then put me into school to qualify me to become a test pilot.

What do I know after coming out of a four-months-a-year school? I have a degree in social science. But today I couldn't pass an eighth-grade test, because I never got the fundamentals.

We went to this one-room country-shack school with a potbellied stove in the middle of the floor. The first grade through the eighth grade was in the same room. There were two teachers, Mrs. Atkins and another one. There must have been a hundred of us in one room. We'd sit there and couldn't get anything out of it, because one teacher was talking to one kid and the other kids were hollering and carrying on.

We knew that down not far from where we lived there was a great big school where the white kids went. We used to talk with a kid named Sonny Boy and another named Raymond and another, Johnny Keith. These were white boys, boys we'd grown up with and played with. We knew that for some reason they had a different kind of school. We couldn't understand why we had to go to our old shack and why we couldn't go to their school. But after a few years we found out.

Our school had shingle windows and a shingle top, so you could sit there and watch the sun, and if it was raining it'd rain down on you. Mrs. Atkins would send Medgar and me and Henry, W. J. and Cloyce, out for pine timber to build a fire. We'd get back from the woods about ten-thirty and it'd be about eleven o'clock before we'd get a good fire going. The other kids would be all huddled up in their old coats the white folks had worn out and given them. Some of the girls would bring old blankets to keep their feet from freezing. Maybe we would have a little spelling or a little reading, but we were too cold to study very much. Even the teacher was cold.

Then about three o'clock we'd start walking that long three miles back home, walking down the dirty road, or in the mud and sloshing rain, and the same white kids that Momma and other Negro mothers had taken care of— would again drive by in their great big shiny yellow and black school bus. And they'd lean out the windows and shout, "Let's see you run, niggers!" And the white bus driver would cut at us and make us jump off the road.

We'd get real mad about it, and Medgar and I began to wait for them. We'd arm ourselves with rocks and hide in the bushes and start a crossfire. I'd get maybe a hundred feet from Medgar on the left side of the road and he'd get on the right side. When they'd pass me I'd throw a rock and run, and when they'd get to where Medgar was stashed he'd throw a rock. This way they didn't know what was going on and they'd speed up because they were afraid to stop. So we found out then that white bullies weren't so big and bad, that they were cowards, and that all they wanted to do was take advantage of us and keep us scared of them.

From the time we were babies, Medgar and I were always roommates. Our room was right at the back of the big old frame house that's still in Decatur. We always had to be in the house by sundown, and Dad would make us go to bed by seven or eight o'clock. We'd go to our room, put on our sleepers—which were unionsuits—then come back in our night clothes and kiss Momma and Daddy. Then we'd go back to our room and close the door and crawl out the back window and go to our "hideout" down by the washhole.

Each Saturday night, Henry McIntosh or Frank Jordan (Frank Jordan is married to my sister Liz) had to steal some lard, Junior Gardner or Cloris Tims had to bring a skillet, and Archie Lee Tims furnished the bread, and Medgar and I furnished the meat—one of Mrs. Atkins' chickens which we'd steal. So we'd make our chicken fry, and we'd be playing and plotting. Then we'd ease back in about midnight and go to bed.

In the winter months the Mississippi dampness really gnaws your bones, and our house was full of cracks. Daddy used to call Medgar and me every morning about five to get up and make a fire. "Charley? Charley? *Charley!*" Then: *"Medgar!"*

"Sir?"

"Git up and make a fire."

"Yes, sir!" And we'd take one foot out of bed and stomp on the old bare wood floor like we were getting out of bed and then lay there another ten minutes.

"Charley? *Charley!*"

"Yes, sir!" And then the same thing. We'd get right back in bed. So finally one morning we'd done that a couple of

times and gone back to sleep when suddenly—*Bang! Bang!*
—Daddy was hitting us with his double razor strop. Man!
We hit that floor! And ran. From then on we jumped
when he called us to make a fire.

We didn't have hot-and-cold-running water. We didn't
even have a well. We had to go down a hill, to a spring,
and we carried the water in buckets back up the hill.
(Later, when I went into the houses of white folks, I saw
that they had hot-and-cold-running water. And I saw that
they didn't use tin tubs for bathing. They had big enamel
tubs.)

But lots of people, especially in the South, were born
poor, and being poor wasn't what hurt. The main thing
was the way white people treated us. How they'd almost
deny us the right just to exist. Momma'd come home tired
and worked down. And then she'd have to wash for the
white folks. She'd have ten or fifteen shirts and all the rest
of the laundry. She'd put the laundry on her head and
Medgar and I'd have our arms full, and she'd say, "Now,
boys, be careful, don't wrinkle Mr. Gaines' shirts. Mr.
Gaines will get mad if you wrinkle his shirts." So we'd
get to the house and we couldn't go in the front door. We
had to go around and come up the back steps, and we
couldn't go any further than the dining room. We'd stand
there and watch Mrs. Gaines hand my mother a lousy 50¢
for washing and ironing fifteen or twenty shirts, overalls
and coveralls, sox and underclothes, and ten or fifteen
sheets. We were just kids, but we vowed we'd be buried in
hell three times if we ever grew up and allowed our youngsters to go through all that. Momma had washed the
white folks' dirty clothes, made their dirty beds, fixed
their food, combed the little nappy-headed children's hair,
and we weren't good enough to come to the front door.
Sometimes Momma'd go and work five or six long days
and they'd give her no more than $2.50 a week.

[46]

Medgar and I asked Momma and Daddy all the time, "Why do we have to do like this?" And they'd say, "It's because we're colored, son." And Medgar and I'd say to each other, "Listen, we're gonna *take* somethin' from them white folks. We're not gonna let them do that to us."

At this time, Medgar and I were picking up pecans for a white widow woman named Mrs. Pace. We'd work all day and pick up three or four bushels and she'd give us some pecans in a child's play bucket for our pay. We'd thank her and go home. Medgar and I'd get our little wagon that we'd made ourselves and late at night we'd go back to Mrs. Pace's barn and get the three or four bushels of pecans we'd picked up and carry them on home. Then with innocent faces we'd go back to Mrs. Pace's the next afternoon to pick up more pecans.

"Charles," she'd say. "You know, somebody stole those pecans last night. Some low-down, dirty scoundrel stole those pecans. And after you boys worked so hard!"

I said, "I'll tell you what, we're gonna fix it so nobody can git in."

She said, "All right, you go and fix it."

We nailed up the door—but tore a plank off one side of the barn. We picked up more bushels of pecans, and again she filled the child's bucket for our pay. That night we went back over there and climbed through the side where we'd left off the plank and hauled off all the bushels of pecans in our wagon. Medgar wanted us to quit while the quitting was good. His nerves were getting thin, but I didn't care. I figured the white folks like Mrs. Pace weren't paying me nothing, so I was going to show them they weren't so smart. "C'mon," I told Medgar. "We're gonna take these pecans down to the pecan man and sell all of 'em."

We changed sacks so he wouldn't know where we'd

gotten them, and we hauled all the pecans we'd stolen from Mrs. Pace to this white pecan-buyer McMillan. He operated from a little store, but had papershells, in bushel bags, scattered out all over the sidewalk, and in a shed, which he never locked. McMillan paid us 3¢ a pound for pecans, but he cheated us on the scales. Maybe we'd have 200 pounds of pecans, but the way he weighed them it'd just show a hundred pounds. There wasn't anything we could do about it. We knew that if we said anything he'd beat us or have us lynched. So we decided we'd just go and steal them off him that night.

A couple of nights later we sneaked back to McMillan's with our wagon and hauled off several bushels of pecans and hid them in some tall grass near home. The next day we put them in some different sacks and took the same pecans back to the old man and resold them to him. We kept doing this and found out that white folks are kinda dumb. They never thought Negro boys would have the nerve to steal their pecans. They always thought some white folks took them.

Once we gave a friend, Robert Smith, Daddy's straight razor and waited at night while he slashed open all McMillan's bags of pecans, scattering them all over. Early the next morning we went back there to hear him cussing and asking Medgar and me if we had any idea of what white scoundrel would be that mean.

I learned from this and other times too many to mention that the criminal always feels he has to return to the scene of the crime. We used to as kids. When the older fellows used to come by to see our sisters, we'd pound big spikes into four-by-fours and lay them under their car tires and just wait. Sometimes all four tires would go at once: Beeyew! Pow] Sleeyew! Spesshhhhhhhhh! We'd always be nearby to see it happen.

[48]

Right here in Fayette a boy broke into the drugstore down by the post office and made off with a couple of TV sets, some cigarettes, things like that. He had picked the lock, then got the stuff out through the back window. Maybe I was lucky, but I told my men to stake out the store the next morning. Nobody said a word. A boy came by, went over and peered in the window. We nabbed him and he confessed.

I wouldn't want anybody to get the idea that the mischief we got into when we were kids, or when my dad was young, is something I'm recommending today. Times are different today. Remember, we had nothing else to do. Today kids have bowling alleys, tennis courts, swimming pools, basketball courts, libraries you can read in, movies, television.

We did what we did for fun. Nowadays kids seem to be bent on destroying. There are other things they can do for fun. At most we might have had a BB gun, or an older teenager might have a .22. But pistols? *Unheard* of! I don't know what's got into kids today that they want to carry guns in their pockets and go shooting and killing each other. Insanity.

We've had our trouble in Fayette since I became Mayor. A fight's a fight, no matter who's Mayor. Once you start drinking whiskey, you get high and start to react. That's why we close the whole town down at 1 o'clock. Just pull the streets in. That goes for everybody's place, including the Evers' place. And only authorized personnel carry weapons of any kind here. If you're caught with a gun in Fayette it'll cost you $100 the first time. The second time it's $300. And you don't get the gun back either.

For whatever reason, crime is way down in Fayette. Folks pay attention to those speeding signs now. Nobody insults anybody. You won't hear any vulgarity in our

[49]

streets, certainly no racial slurs on anybody, white or black. And the young people are getting taught how to behave properly. You won't find any bunch of kids playing around out of school. Not in Fayette, you won't.

5

Decatur, 1933–34

Every fall we'd kill a hog and we'd cut it up and salt it down. The night before eating it, Momma would take it out and put it in water to try to soak some of the salt out of it. She should have known that to soak out the salt she'd need to keep changing the water, but she'd leave it soaking in the same salty water all night. And then in the morning she'd take the meat out of the water, rinse it off and put it right into the frying pan. The hog meat would twirl up just like a meatskin, and when you'd try to eat it, it'd be so salty it would just lock your jaw!

Momma always saw that we got enough to eat. It wasn't always the things we wanted to eat, but she'd manage one way or another. We had a garden. We raised okra, black-eyed peas, potatoes and corn. And Momma would can all of these during the fall.

When Momma baked cookies, I'd tell Medgar they'd

taste better if we stole them. Momma would cook them and put them up on a big wooden platter. And as fast as Momma cooked two or three batches we'd go and steal five or six or ten of them, so when she'd cooked three batches she'd find she had no more than when she started and she'd call out, "What happened to these cookies?"

And I'd say, "I don't know, Momma. I don't know."

"Charles, don't lie to me! Come here!"

Medgar and I'd go in there—"Open your mouth!"—and she'd see all the crumbs. She'd slap our faces and go get Daddy's double razor strop. "Now, listen," she'd say. "It's wrong to tell a story. If you lie about this you lie about somethin' else." She'd beat the stew out of me.

When Momma whipped Medgar and me, she'd say, "I'm praying the Lord will give me strength to whip your behind!" She meant that, and boy, she'd lay it on. She wasn't just praying and talking about how "the Lord is gonna take care of you." No! She'd beat the devil out of you, and keep praying while she was at it.

I always wanted to be first. "Let me get mine over with." Oh, I was stubborn. I wouldn't holler for nothing. Momma'd beat me almost down and I'd just stand there and take it. Momma or Daddy neither one could make me cry.

I had a shaggy brown dog named Trim I'd trained to protect me, and Momma could never whip me out in the yard, because Trim would jump on her. If Momma was beating me outside she had to stop and tie Trim up on the inside, and then he'd be yelping and carrying on trying to get out and protect me.

Momma'd wear herself out on me, so she'd have to rest awhile and then take Medgar on. He'd start crying before you hit him. He'd jump, scream, holler and run. I'd be sitting there laughing at him, and then Momma would chase after me. She'd rap me across the shoulder and make me get out of the room, so I'd go outside and start pestering my sister Liz. We took it out on her because she always tattled on Medgar and me.

There was no swimming pool, so we'd go down by the railroad tracks to the washhole and go swimming there. We used to have little girls swimming with their little brothers, and Medgar and I'd fool the little brothers into going under the water while we kissed their little sisters. We'd all be naked, you know. We thought that was something. I must have been ten or eleven. God, that was a long time ago, but it doesn't seem like it. We'd play "hiding." The brothers would count while we hid in the bushes with the little girls. We'd stick them a bit between their legs and run. And the white girls would come play with us. We'd call it screwing them, but we really wasn't doing nothing.

In school, Medgar was the bookworm. He was much smarter than any of the rest of us. He studied harder. He'd sit out on our back porch for hours, reading. He was easygoing, wasn't loud like I was (and still am). And he wasn't disliked as I am. I think it was because I always had to have my say. I just wouldn't back up. I was always very blunt and to the point, which is not always the best way to be. I was the "loud-mouthed" Evers boy. And I was always hustling. One thing I know, and that's how to make money. From the very beginning I could make money. I'd try to find Coke bottles and sell them for a penny apiece. I'd hustle scrap iron. I'd scour the fields and all the nearby towns for old plows and odd pieces discarded from the construction of railroads. I had to pick up about 100 pounds of scrap iron to make a dime, but I made a little money that way. And I'd press cigarette foil out and sell it and make a few pennies that way.

A boy named Leon Eatman (he later went to live in New York) started calling me *Dermp* because an ol' white peddler by that name would come across the tracks and sell Bibles and mail-order shoes and cheap mirrors and all kinds of things to the Negroes. I got stuck with that name, Dermp the peddler. And I just hated peddlers. But I guess I had a bit of the peddler in me. Those old white peddlers would come around and never knock on the door, just walk right on in and sit on the side of the bed with a "I'm yo Raleigh man" or whatever the case might be. "Watcha need today?" And Medgar and I'd get so mad at the way they conned our people into buying their junk that while they were in the house we'd slip around and unscrew all the bolts on their truck wheels. He'd waste all his watermelons and peaches—they'd burst all in the middle of the road. And the old Watkins man would sell all those flavors, spices, vanilla and others. He'd have big boxes of black pepper, overselling it by about three prices. We'd fool him. He'd come up to our place and we'd say, "Miz so and so down in the pastures wants some black pepper," and he'd take off down there with the black pepper and leave his truck. Then we'd clean him out. We'd get all of whatever he had in his truck and dump it out on the ground.

Momma, like all the black womenfolks, didn't give a damn what the man was selling, she was going to buy it—brushes, Bibles, tonics. You name it. And most black women did that. Most of the stores were far away and they had to get dressed to go to town. And they didn't have any clothes fit to go to town. The peddlers would let them have their junk on credit. But you better pay them or they'd take you out and give you a good butt-whipping, or do something to somebody. So the peddlers weren't worried about getting their money. They'd come in and sit on the bed and cross their legs, cozylike. And what made me so angry was that I couldn't go to a white woman's house without going to the back door and standing around outside. Yet this white man would come in our front door, without knocking, and sit on our bed. And nobody in there but our mother.

When Medgar and I tried to sell newspapers the whites said, "No, that's a job for white boys." So I said to Medgar, "If we can't sell to them, why should they sell to us?" And sometimes when a white boy'd come down there we'd jump out from the bushes and throw a toe-sack over his head and pull the drawstrings and grab all the papers away from him and throw them all out through the woods. And by the time he got untangled from the sack we'd be gone. But when we'd throw him down, we'd tell him, "If we can't sell papers in your neighborhood, you can't sell papers in our neighborhood." So we broke that up, at least for a while.

Then you had white peddlers selling peaches, pecans, watermelons, eggs, chickens and old beef they hadn't purified, hadn't washed hardly. And there was the Lotts furniture man who'd go around selling us all of their broken-down furniture. When the Lotts furniture man would come in and park his truck and go into people's houses, we'd dig holes under his truck and bury our old reliable two-by-fours with big spikes and cover them right under his tires where he had to back over them. When he backed it up—*spewwwwing!*—the tires would go flat.

There was ol' man Tobe, who peddled eggs and tomatoes. He was always around, knew everything, couldn't nobody tell him anything. He knew all about the white folks and all about the black folks, everybody's business— who was where and who was going with who. And every Saturday morning old man Tobe used to come down to where we lived with his eggs in a basket on his head. Medgar and I'd try to get our people not to buy eggs from him, but they'd buy them anyway. "You Evers boys gonna git in trouble messin' with these white folks. Yo'll too biggity," they'd say. They were scared. I used to say to Medgar, "Those ol' crazy Negroes should be ashamed, those white folks ain't nothin'. They ain't no more than nobody else. But they're scared of 'em. I bet I ain't scared, of none of 'em."

This Tobe man would come through there singing and humming, and in those days Tarzan was very popular. We used to listen to him on the radio and see him in the movies. We had a little buzzard-roof movie we'd go to and we'd see how Tarzan would dig all his ditches and make all his traps—he could whip all the Negroes and all the apes and all the tigers, all everything. I never could figure that out, either. Medgar and I said, "We gonna fix ol' man Tobe."

We went out into the woods at night and dug a hole about five feet wide and three feet deep and filled it up with straw, pine needles, oak leaves and covered dirt over the top. The hole was right in his path; he couldn't miss it. The next morning we were up in a tree when he came. He went right to the hole and went down, his eggs going one way and his tomatoes the other. We slid down the tree and took off. But he recognized us and told Momma, and she whipped us.

But we didn't stop there. We had a cow pasture, so we'd get a shovel and haul cow manure and spread it along the path, and we spread more than one pile. We used pine needles and oak leaves. We did these things all because they were white. But Momma kept saying that poor old Tobe could have broken his neck. So we began to realize that maybe we were a little wrong. But that didn't stop us.

Robert Smith was one of the bad boys. He'd steal. He was bigger and older than the rest of us, and he'd pick on us. He was the kind you liked to be around, but you knew that one day he was going to tear you apart. Robert was the big bully in our community. Every boy is in awe of

[56]

power, and the bully represented power to us. We didn't like him too well, but we had no choice. Medgar and I'd never fight fair. We'd always double-team on them. And we wouldn't just fight with our hands. We'd get sticks and bricks and bats. All of us had to be home by sundown, so about sundown we'd start watching Robert because we knew he was going to do something stupid—like, hit one of us and run, or get down the road and throw a rock at us. A whole gang of us would get ready and start picking on Robert, trying to get the jump on him and make him run off. He'd knock us down, but we'd get up and come after him. One day Robert was picking on Medgar, so later I said to Medgar, "We're gonna fix ol' Robert Smith."

Daddy's Baptist church was about a half a mile from the spring where we'd get water. When I saw Robert outside the church before Sunday school, I told him, "You dirty rascal, you hit Medgar. I'm gonna beat you."

"What!" he said.

"C'mon down to the spring with me."

Meantime, I'd told Medgar to go down there and hide behind a bush, that I was going to fool Robert down there. The rest of the boys had hid behind trees. Robert followed me down to the spring, and I pushed him—if he'd had any sense at all he would have known something was wrong—and he swung. Then I flew into him and held him, and while I was holding him Medgar came out from behind that bush with a baseball bat and clobbered him. Robert was tumbled up in a heap. It's a wonder we didn't kill him. After we'd clobbered him we jumped on him and beat him until one of the boys had to pull us off him. He was as bloody as a hog. He jumped up crying "I'm gonna tell my daddy and I'm gonna get his gun." We took off to get our guns. Everybody had rifles, everybody hunted. But someone had reported at the church that we were fighting, and as we were running up the hill we met the preacher, Reverend Witherspoon, Mr. Clarence Tims and Mr. Willie Warnsley came after us. They grabbed us and whipped us, and we ran home and Daddy beat the tar out of us. Robert got a beating from his grandfather after he had gotten a beating from us. And Frank Jordan's dad whipped Frank and made him stay in the house all day.

The next Sunday we decided we'd get into more mischief because there was a mean white man who used to raise some great big watermelons near the church. He was named Harris, and we wanted to get even with him. We went to Sunday school this time, and when it was over we took off for Harris's watermelon patch. We were going to steal the watermelons and take them to our hideout, but someone must have tipped Harris off, because he was hid in the bushes with his shotgun. When we started stealing he started shooting. We took off like rabbits—and nobody got caught, except Frank. Frank's daddy was a section hand working for the railroad and they lived in one of those section houses. In those days we had this high iron bed that you could almost stand up under. Frank's daddy made Frank get under that bed. This was about one o'clock—and *hot!* He made him stay under there till eight o'clock that night.

Medgar and I were running around by the window, peeping in and taunted him, "Hey, Frank, come here."

"You know I can't come from under here."

We teased him until Mister Jordan heard it and came out so we took off. But Mister Jordan told our daddy and our daddy made us get under our bed, and we stayed under the bed all that evening and all that night, sleeping on the floor as punishment for trying to steal Harris's watermelons.

Medgar loved to hunt and fish, but I got very sensitive about killing. One night I went 'possum hunting with some grown men and we saw this 'possum; the dogs had treed the 'possum. We threw a light on him and it blinded the poor 'possum. A man took a stick and beat his brains out. That bothered me. I think maybe it was because that 'possum had life, and his life was just as sweet to him as mine to me. I guess I sort of related that to somebody beating my brains out. And I ran. I just started running, and they didn't know what happened. But I never went hunting after that. I never liked killing rabbits, or even a bird. Medgar was different. He was a hunter and fisherman.

I was about ten and Medgar about eight when local whites in Decatur killed one of our father's friends, Willie Tingle. Mr. Tingle was supposed to have looked at a white woman, or insulted her. They dragged him through the streets behind a wagon and hung him up to a tree and shot at him.

Later, when I was a grown man, I'd go back to Decatur and see these same white folks who killed Mr. Tingle. One of them was drying up like a seed. I thought: He must remember the night he and the other hate-mongers killed Mister Tingle.

The way they treated him really got Medgar and me bitter toward white people. We knew we had to do something about it.

6

Decatur, Forest, Newton, 1935–36

As kids in Decatur, Medgar and I played with white children, mostly belonging to the folks Momma used to work for, like Frank Gaines. There were Margaret Gaines and Bobby Gaines, the Hollingworth kids, Sonny Boy Jordan and some others. We all grew up together, we played together, we slept on the same pallet, so we had to be a part of each other. And we loved each other as kids. We knew that we were black and white, but not to the point that we could even think about it. We used to play without any problems until we started growing up. One day Momma was going to the Gaineses and we said, "Momma, we wanna go too, we wanna play with Margaret and Bobby."

But Momma said, "No, you can't go and play with them no more."

"Why, Momma?"

They didn't tell us these things. I know now that Mrs.

Gaines must have told Momma, "Jessie, you know Margaret's growing up now, and I think it's time you told Charles and Medgar . . ." She didn't have to draw any pictures. Momma understood. It's always been that way in the South. When Momma talked to us about Margaret Gaines it was in a way we couldn't understand: "Margaret can't run and jump," or "You can't see Margaret no more, you can't beat on Margaret no more, 'cause she's a big girl now. And you can't play with her like you used to."

Sometime later, Liz or Medgar or I would meet Margaret Gaines on the road, going to town, and she'd stop and talk. She always showed that she'd never forgotten we'd played together as kids and had been friends. But she was different from most of the rest.

When I was about twelve and Medgar ten, our half-brother Eddie, Momma's son, was about twenty-eight. I guess I admired Eddie because he was adventurous. He was kind of wild, a hobo. He was very courteous, didn't sass Momma, but he'd just go and couldn't nobody stop him. And I sort of admire people you can't control. Back in those days, Momma would knock you down if you were forty years old if you even looked at her the wrong way. But Eddie was something else. He'd tell Medgar and me about where he'd been and what was going on. That's why you have to be very careful. Some young people will idolize you. I don't care *what* you're doing, hoboing, taking dope, stealing of *what*. Somebody's going to idolize you— like we did Eddie. The more people talk about something, the more enthused you get over it, the more you want to see and do it. I think that's one thing that pushed us to go and see what the world was like.

Eddie'd catch trains, so we'd catch trains, too. We'd catch them right there at home—the tracks ran just back of our house. We'd slip off and go to Newton and Union.

Once we were going to Newton but the train didn't stop in Newton and we were heading into Laurel. The train was going so fast, we didn't know how we'd get off. We were getting too far from home and we didn't have money. We knew the old yard man was rough on hobos, and we knew what would happen if he caught us—he'd put us in jail, or something worse. The moment we jumped off he saw us and started after us. We ran. Oh man, did we run. We got over to the highway and hitchhiked and got home the next day.

Momma didn't know where we'd been, and Daddy thought we'd run off. Daddy said, "You're runnin' off because you ain't got nothin' to do! You're *idlesome*." And he beat the stew out of us. He said, "I'm gonna give you somethin' to do!" And he worked us hard the rest of the summer.

Eddie didn't travel very far, but as boys Medgar and I thought any place away from Decatur was as far away as the moon. Eddie would just go around in Mississippi, but that was more than anyone else I knew ever did. Until my baby sister Ruth died in Chicago, my daddy had never left Mississippi in his life. There are people in Mississippi who've never been to Jackson. Thousands of them. And yet I'm really not saying anything. I'm sure there are thousands who live in Virginia and have never been to Washington, D.C. But you'd just sort of think that everybody in Mississippi would go to Jackson. Well, it's the only town in Mississippi that has a zoo. When we were kids it was a great thing to go to Jackson.

I remember the first time I went to Jackson. I was about twelve and I ran off from home. I'd never sass my people, I'd just leave. In Jackson I got a job in a white café. In those days they didn't have no phones, so Momma and Daddy didn't know where I was for two weeks. Other people had phones, but my people didn't. So Momma and

Daddy worried, and Momma prayed. I stayed with a woman named Mrs. Tims—a black Mrs. Tims, not the white one I was telling about earlier. I stayed with her until Daddy found out and made me come home.

Soon after this Eddie came home and got sick, with a severe headache, and in that small town we knew nothing about X-rays. He was afraid to go to the hospital. So from the way he suffered and from the reactions now we think it must have been cancer of the brain. After Eddie died I didn't want to do anything. Momma couldn't get me to eat. But I didn't cry. I'd sit out on our back porch and watch every freight that came by. I guess I kept thinking Eddie might be on one of them.

We kept moving around because there wasn't a school worth a dime in Decatur, and so at various times we were in Decatur, Newton and Forest. Forest is about twenty miles west of Newton, and Newton is twenty miles south of Decatur. In Forest I lived with one of my uncles, Mark Thomas. He was my great-great-uncle and the one who reared my daddy.

There were two or three girls that Medgar and I grew up with in Decatur, but there was a girl by the name of Ruby Nelle Willis in Newton that I fell in love with when I was about twelve. Ruby Nelle lived with her Negro mother, but she was like a white girl—almost. Her daddy was a white man. He lived not too far from our house in Decatur. Her daddy didn't deny Ruby Nelle. White men in Mississippi usually deny their children by Negro women, but not always. Sometimes they brag about it—"I got my nigger children"—and "I got a nigger woman down the street." The same way the old plantation owners did.

I've asked myself if I fell in love with Ruby Nelle because she was light-skinned. Most Negroes back in those days were brainwashed by the whites into thinking the light-skinned girls were prettier than the dark-skinned.

[63]

Later on I fell in love with Virgene Williams, who was dark. So I think I loved Ruby because she was Ruby, sweet and affectionate Ruby. I'll never forget Ruby.

While I was in high school one of the white Tims boys who'd grown up with me in Decatur was working in the Newton bank. One day I went in there and called him by his first name and he looked at me real funny and said, "Listen, James Charles, you call me *mister.*"

"What?"

"You call me *mister.*"

I got mad, and I was hurt. This was the same boy I'd known all my life. We'd played together, grown up together, gone swimming together, sat and pulled cockle-burrs out of our feet together—and he was telling me to call him *mister.* I told Medgar about it. He was always quiet and understanding. He said, "Well, Charley, that's just the way white folks are. He thinks now you're supposed to call him mister."

"Like hell I'm gonna call him mister. I'm never going to call anybody mister, either. I'm a man. I'm just as grown as he is. In fact, I'm older. Why should I call him mister?"

"Well," I said, "are you going to call me mister?"

When I went back home I told Momma and Daddy about it. And they said, "Well, that's just the way white people are. They think they're better than we are."

There were a couple of white men I knew who worked part-time around the bus station, and I told one of them about it, and he said, "When you get a certain age, you're supposed to honor and respect the white man."

"Well," I said, "are you going to call me mister?"

And he said, "No, you don't call *Negroes* mister."

I said, "I won't call you mister, either."

Medgar and I were going to school in Newton because I had a job working in the bus-station café there. A white woman, Mrs. Payne, was the manager. I stayed in her house and she partially reared me and Medgar. Mrs. Payne was someone I could talk to. She'd say, "Look, son. You're just as good as anybody. Always remember that."

The café had one kitchen, but two sides to eat from, one for whites, one for blacks. One day I was in the kitchen fixing hamburgers when some drunk came in. I carried a hamburger over to him and he called me a "dirty black nigger" and started cursing me. Mrs. Payne heard him and lit into him. "Listen! I won't have you bothering Charles. He works for me, and if you don't like it you get out of here!"

The drunk said something like, "Well, he must be your black lover boy."

And she said, "He's my black son. And don't you mess with him. He's working here and he's doing what I tell him."

He cursed me again and she ordered him out of the café, and he left.

When I went back to the kitchen I was really angry. I'd peek out to see who was coming in, and if he was one of those racists, bigots or hate-mongers I'd spit in his hamburger or scrambled eggs four or five times and say, "Now, you dirty white rascal, you can curse me, but you're eatin' some of my spit!" And I'd send it on out to him and watch him eat it.

White people have got to understand that they've got to help us not to hate. Because whatever we are, white people made us that. And I don't bite no bones about it. They've given us no reason to love. All they've ever done, since the time we were little boys, is just create problems for us. And give us reasons to hate and want to kill. But thank God people like Mrs. Payne kept Medgar and me from becoming fanatics. She was a good woman and knew right from wrong.

7

When Medgar and I were growing up the Klan was in its heyday, but it never came into our neighborhood. We were called "those crazy niggers"—whenever a black man was outspoken he was considered "crazy" or "dangerous" —and the crazy niggers of Mississippi never had too much trouble out of the white folks because they knew if they killed any of us, we were going to kill some of them. There were always some who just wouldn't take it.

On Christmas Eve the Kluxers didn't allow Negroes to come into town. They'd be there shooting Roman candles, sparklers and firecrackers. Daddy had made Medgar and me a baseball bat out of a broom handle that had a tap on the end of it. "C'mon, boys," he said. "We're goin' to town. If anyone throws a firecracker we're gonna use this on him."

We walked down the street, white folks staring at us and

Daddy swinging that homemade baseball bat. A white boy ran up in front of us and Daddy told him, "You throw that firecracker and I'll bust your brains out." The boy ran and told his daddy, and my daddy said to the white man, "That goes for you, too!" Somehow or other, they didn't bother us. And I don't know why, because for a nigger in those day to tell a white man "I'll bust your brains out"— well, you were automatically dead. Then Daddy told this white man, "And you better not come to our house, either."

We went on and did our shopping and daddy told the shop owner what happened, and the owner said to the white men who were standing around in there, "You leave Jim alone. You get on away from here. Leave Jim alone." And they didn't bother us. We went on home, but Medgar and I thought the Klan was coming for sure, so we told Daddy, "We better sit up tonight." And Daddy said, "That's right." And we did, along with two friends, Henry and W. J. Roosevelt.

Our house was the last one on the road leading from town, and anyone who got to our house had to come right down that road. Medgar and I went down the road, toward town, with our rifles. And sat waiting for them. We were hoping they would come and we stayed up till sunrise. We got up and walked down the road with our rifles, and all our neighbors saw us. They had all heard about what had happened and were scared. But we were disappointed. We had waited all night for them, and if they'd come we'd have killed every last one of them because they couldn't have seen us. We were in the dark.

Medgar and I had begun to hate. Every night Momma prayed for us. She'd always try to tell us that hatred only breeds more hatred. We couldn't see it then. White hate-mongers all over Mississippi put up signs in all their towns: NEGRO, READ. IF YOU CAN'T READ, RUN

ANYHOW. And if the Negro didn't run, they'd catch him and beat him. Every family could tell you these scary tales of what had happened to some black father or brother or son. During this time a Negro boy was killed by whites who claimed he'd attacked a white woman, which was a lie. That Negro boy didn't attack a white woman! In those days—and I don't mind saying it—it was the white women who attacked the young Negroes. They were always making trouble. Medgar and I—and I say it with reservation—had more trouble getting away from white girls than we did with Negro girls. I know a couple of white girls in Decatur and every time I see them we sort of smile. I wonder if they're thinking what I'm thinking. When they were fifteen and sixteen every chance they'd get they'd just pull at us and bother us. Decatur was a small, dull place, so I guess they wanted some excitement. But they knew they'd be protected—because they were white. And I guess it gave them a thrill to see how scared of them we were. I'll never forget when I was about thirteen I went to Hattiesburg and got a job washing dishes. I was scared because of this white girl, a waitress. She'd come in every morning while I'd be washing dishes and she'd just stand over me, and let her breasts hit me in the back. She'd pretend she was getting something and rub herself all up against me. *And I was scared to death.* I asked her not to do that. But she kept on, so I quit.

A white woman used to ask Medgar or me to wash her windows. We couldn't wash them without her pulling on our arms or legs. I'd be washing her windows and she'd pull on my leg and want me to come down: "Show me if you're a man or still a little boy." When we told Momma about her, she said to stay out of her way, so we never worked for her any more.

So you see, it disturbs me when white men kill a Negro about some white woman. In most cases, but not all, she has bothered *him*. There's many a black man buried because a white woman didn't have the guts to say, "Yes, I asked him. You leave him alone."

In Canton, police said a fourteen-year-old Negro boy was telephoning a white girl, so they took him out and nearly beat him to death. The boy was calling the daughter of a sheriff, by a black woman. (White men go in for nighttime integration, backdoor integration, cottonfield integration. They work black women all day and become intimate with them all night.) They killed Emmett Till. Ollie Shelby looked at a white woman, so the deputy sheriff shot him in the head. They killed a Negro boy in Port Gibson. Then they cut his privates off and dragged him up near the sheriff's house and left him in the middle of the road. Also in Port Gibson, they found a black boy drowned with his hands tied behind his back. They didn't give a reason, didn't have to give a reason in Mississippi. To kill a nigger, or a nigger-lover, wasn't anything.

8

Decatur, 1936–39

Daddy always insisted that Medgar and I work, so he bought a couple of mules for us to use on various jobs, like hauling lumber and pulling the grinding wheel at a sugarmill. The mules were named Kate and Maud. Whatever was to be done we used Maud. We'd work her in the fields all day and ride her home for dinner. With old Maud you could crawl all up between her legs, you could grab her back feet and raise a foot to look at her shoe, and she'd never kick you. We worked Maud and rode Maud and did everything to Maud. But Kate was a mean one! She'd kick the sweetening out of gingerbread and never crack the crust. She wouldn't let you ride her for nothing, and if you tried she'd kick you to kingdom-come. So we'd feed her and leave her alone, and Kate was always rested, and was always respected and always did exactly what Kate wanted to do. This taught me something about being humble and submissive. The easier you are, the more people use you.

Medgar and I'd ride Maud to a sugarmill where the white people were making syrup for the winter. They'd hire us to work and to use Maud. We'd harness Maud to a wheel to grind the cane and she'd walk round and round in a circle all day. We'd help the grownups throw in the cane to be squeezed and mashed, and we'd see the juice flowing into a strainer that strained away the shucks. Then it went into a cooker, and after it cooked four or five hours the syrup would be poured into five-gallon cans for market. After we'd worked all day and worked Maud all day, the white folks wouldn't pay us any money. They'd give us one little bucket of syrup. We knew what they were giving us wasn't enough. So at night I'd say, "C'mon, Medgar, let's go get our pay." And we'd slip back down there and carry off one or two of those five-gallon cans of syrup.

Whatever nickel or dime or quarter Medgar or I made, we saved. We'd clean out a Bull Durham chewing-tobacco sack and keep our money in it. Medgar would crawl up under his side of the bed and tie his little sack to the springs and I'd tie mine on my side of the bed. We weren't allowed to go on each other's side. Later, Daddy gave us a little dime bank you could only put dimes in. We'd work every evening after school trying to get us a dime. Every dime we got we put in that bank. We had a game to see who would fill up that bank quicker. This is the way we saved our money, and our Momma and Daddy never knew what we had, because if they had found it, they would want to know where we were getting it, and we were getting a lot of it by stealing.

I had a cousin there in Decatur called T-Boy, and T-Boy and I—we must have been about fourteen—got a job racking oakwood up four feet high and eight feet long. We were hired by the sawmill at 10¢ an hour. The first day, I saw how whites kicked Negroes just because they didn't jump when they told them.

Both of us were just learning what we were supposed to do, and a white man shouted at T-boy and kicked him completely off the ramp. I lost control of myself and ran over to that white man and I shouted, "Why did you kick T-Boy? If you kick me, *I'll kill you.*" We stood there glaring at each other. He didn't kick me either. I saw he was nothing but a bully—and a coward. I realized that these rednecked whites only attack those who will allow them to attack them. This convinced me that if you just stand for what's right and don't bow one way or the other, you'll be able to do the things you want to do and you'll be able to make it a better place.

My daddy was a lumber-stacker at this mill, and the white devil who'd kicked T-Boy ran to him and said, "You better talk to James Charles. He's talkin' 'bout killin' me."

Daddy asked, "Charles, did you say that?"

"Yes, sir, I sure did. And I meant it, Daddy. If he kicks me like he kicked T-Boy, I'll kill him. I'll go get my rifle and kill him."

"You go on home, Charley. You go on home, go on home."

He made me go home, and I didn't work at the sawmill any more. Don't *nobody* kick me.

About this same time a white man named Cooper hired Medgar and me at 10¢ an hour to haul lumber by truck from Decatur to Lake, round-trip. That's about forty miles. We would work ten hours a day for a dollar a day. We'd load 2 x 12's on the truck in Decatur and unload them in Lake. Cooper worked us six days, Monday through Saturday night, and he didn't pay us anything. He never gave us any excuse. He just didn't pay us. When I told Daddy, he said, "Charles, the man says he ain't got it."

"Didn't they pay him for the lumber?"

"Yeah," he said. "But what can we do? Ol' Cooper's a mean man."

And I said, "Let me tell you somethin'. I ain't never gonna work for any white folks any more!"

A few years later this same man was in Jackson, selling cars. I found him, and I went to him and asked for my money, and he wouldn't pay me. I said, "I better not catch nobody buyin' no car from you, I bet you that."

I must have been about fourteen when I started noticing that Daddy wasn't staying home all the time. The boy and the girl whose mother he was spending time with were very close to us, we were all friends, and we always used to see Daddy over there, and I didn't exactly know what his business was. But kids aren't dumb. Later on I realized he was giving that family things. We'd see the other kids wearing new clothes while we had nothing. And I knew we were being denied. So finally Momma explained to us what was going on. And we confronted our Dad, and he denied the charges.

I'll never forget the day Momma discussed another woman with my Dad, how he was neglecting his family economically. He said something sharp to her, and Momma gave him a sharp answer and he threatened her. Medgar and I were sitting around the fire and we stood up. "You better not hit Momma!" we said. Then Medgar went and got a butcher knife and I got the hammer, and I said, "If you hit Momma, I'll kill you."

Well, this sort of problem continued for a while, and after a few years he was the best husband you could find. They lived together until he died. Momma waited it out. So I vowed I'd never give a girl a box of candy, or a valen-

[73]

tine. I never gave one a flower. I didn't give one anything. I felt that women laughed at Daddy, and I didn't want any woman laughing at me. As a result, I haven't been too popular with women. But it doesn't matter. I always felt that I had to work too hard for what I have and I am not about to give it away. Nobody gives you anything. You got to work for it. I promised my mother that my wife would never have to suffer because of some other woman. And no woman is going to come between us. I do little things like any other man—that's to be expected—but nothing will come between us. And I'm not going to come between any other man and his family.

Medgar and I were great admirers of Kenyatta. We read about the Mau Mau killings, and heard about them on the radio. The white people were saying how terrible Kenyatta was, but it was the way the white people told about the cowboys and the Indians—and we were for the Indians and we were for Kenyatta. He was our kind of man, and we wanted to do the kind of things he was doing. We admired Kenyatta so much that we decided at that time if Medgar or me had a son we'd name him after Kenyatta. I don't have a son, but Medgar did—and he named him Darrell Kenyatta.

We were going to organize our own Mau Maus, and nobody was going to know who was killing all the white people. Here's how we were going to do it: When the whites killed a Negro, we'd go to another town, a town where there was a bad sheriff or bad policeman, and one of us would kill that sheriff or policeman. If Medgar was going to do the shooting, I'd drive him to the town and leave him and come back by car. Then he'd take a bus back to keep anybody from suspecting us by seeing us speed away. If I was going to do the killing, he'd drive me to the town and leave me, then I'd come back by bus.

We were going to do all the shootings ourselves. But we

were going to kill a lot of other white people—whole families—by getting Negro maids to poison their food. We thought we had it pretty well worked out. And we thought killing white people would be the only way to ever teach them what's right. But somehow Momma sensed what we were planning to do. We'd bought a lot of bullets for our rifles and when Momma found all this ammunition it scared her. Daddy found it—and he watched us. He wouldn't let us have our rifles unless he was going out with us.

9

Decatur and Forest, 1937–39

Momma used to take in roomers or boarders. I don't care who came along, Momma would take them in. Ed Meyers was one of those slickers who came from Macon and was supposed to be working in Decatur on some kind of construction gang. But Ed was really selling bootleg whisky. He had a nice car, and I wanted to learn how to drive so bad that Ed agreed to teach me. I didn't know Ed was in the liquor business. After he taught me how to drive I'd drive all over the state for him, and if we had been stopped I would have been the one responsible. He'd get in the back seat and lay down and go to sleep, and we'd drive to Forest, Newton and Union, loaded with bootleg whisky, which we call "white lightning." It was made at home out of fermented corn and sugar and an acid we named "devil lye" because it was so strong it would nearly knock you out. When I learned that Ed was selling whisky I didn't say anything. I played along with him. Finally I began to buy whisky where he was buying it. I've always been the kind of guy who feels that if I can do it for you, I can do it for myself.

A man named Ezra Wonley in Decatur sold whisky. Daddy would get so angry over Ezra he'd say, "Ol' Sorry Ezra don't work nowhere, don't do nothin' but bootleg whisky."

Medgar and I would say, "Daddy, he has more than we have. And his children go to school well dressed."

Daddy would say, "You shut up! You shut up!"

Medgar and I'd make blackberry wine and put it in a large jug, stop it up and let it set for three or four weeks until it got strong. We'd sell this wine for a nickel a glass. When we learned where Ezra Wonley hid his whisky we began to steal it. We'd hide it in a ditch behind the house. He sold whisky for 50¢ a pint, but we sold it for a quarter. Bootlegging, we learned, was lucrative.

Later on we began to buy whisky by the gallon from an old white bootlegger. Daddy never knew this. We'd claim we were going fishing, but we'd buy whisky, pour it up in half-pint bottles and take it out in the middle of an open field. We'd sit out on a stump and sell it, and that's why we called it "stump whisky." Sitting out in the open field we could scan in all directions, so the cops never found us.

There were three or four honky-tonks that sold whisky for me. I'd bring them ten to fifty half-pints on a Friday and then I'd go back on Monday and collect my money. If they didn't have my money, they had my whisky. If they didn't have my whisky, they had to account for it. If they didn't account for it, then we had a little session.

People who drank bad bootleg whisky sometimes got what we called the "jake-leg," so people got afraid to drink the whisky and wouldn't anybody buy a bottle unless you "knocked the poison off" by taking one of the first slugs. But I didn't drink, and because I didn't drink the stuff everybody else was afraid to drink it so my business fell off. I found a man who liked to drink and took him with me, and he knocked off the poison for me. He did it just for the drink. He would stand out there with me, and every time someone would come by he'd take a swallow.

Then I went over to Forest to live with my uncle, Mark Thomas, who owns a funeral home. Ed Meyers had taught me to drive, so my uncle had me working at his funeral home picking up bodies. In those days, if you went to a funeral, say, at eleven in the morning, you didn't get back until five or six at night, because everybody shouted and screamed and fell around and tried to get down in the hole with the dead person.

Uncle Mark had an ambulance and a hearse. And whenever I learned that he was gone I'd get in the ambulance and go to Vicksburg, where they sold sealed whisky. I was too young to buy, but I paid off an older man to buy it and carry it to his garage. I'd take Medgar or somebody with me in the ambulance, and when I'd get the whisky I'd hide it under the ambulance bed and make whoever was with me get in the bed and lay down and I'd return with the siren open. I'd come right through all those small towns with the siren blasting. Screaming siren and bootleg whisky. I'd just be rolling and people would be getting out of the way. I'd carry the whisky into Forest about dark, drive up into the shed where we kept the ambulance, pull the door down and run in and get the dead-man cot and unload my whisky on it and carry it into the embalming room. I'd take the embalming fluid aside and start stacking my whisky and put the fluid on top of the whisky.

This way I kept my sealed whisky, scotch, bourbon and gin. I had men who'd sell it for me. If someone wanted fifty half-pints, I'd give them fifty half-pints, and they would sell it and bring the money back. No one could say that I was selling whisky. I was the one backing all the bootleggers. Half-pints of whisky were 75¢ to $1. I'd give the hony-tonk owners a quarter for every half-pint they sold. Therefore, they made about a 25 percent profit on everything they sold. That's a pretty good profit.

Bootlegging is popular because to sell whisky legally you've got to be worth at least $4,000 or $5,000 to get started. How many blacks have that kind of money in Mississippi? Some people still buy whisky and resell it at bootleg prices without a license because they can't afford to buy a license. A liquor license in Mississippi costs $2,000. To acquire some stock costs another $2,000 or $3,000. And to get some help and run a place costs you another $100 a month. A case of whisky can be bought for $60 or $70 and resold for $35 or $40 more. If one makes $35 or $40 that will buy groceries and pay some of the bills for a week.

10

*Decatur, and to Australia, New Guinea,
the Philippines, 1940–46*

When I was growing up, Negroes were barred from the air
corps and the marines so I joined the army when I was
seventeen. It was in 1940, and they paid $21 a month.
God! I wanted to get away from home so bad! There
had been thousands of black boys who joined the army
because anything, even a foxhole, would be better than
what we had. Momma didn't want me to go, but I lied
about my age and signed up. I was sent to Camp Shelby,
at Hattiesburg. When the army found out that I was
underage, they sent me back home. Then I went over to
Forest to work for my Uncle Mark Thomas. When I was
eighteen I signed up at Decatur and went back to Hattiesburg.

At that time the army was segregated, our officers were
white, and they were racists. They didn't call us niggers,
but they did everything but that. They had to call us sol-

diers, but it was the way they said it. The kind of assignments they gave us, and the kind of restrictions we adhered to and the kind of punishment they administered —it's almost unbelievable now.

I was in an all-Negro unit at Hattiesburg about three or four months. We hardly had any food to eat. We had an uncomfortable place to live. The treatment was harsh. It was very difficult for us. You have to experience segregation to know why it is a terrible thing. I came home on furlough and explained to Medgar what it was like. He volunteered, and received the experience, too. We agreed that we would go in the army and learn how to kill white folks. When we were stationed in the army, we found out what a terrible thing it is to kill.

In 1942 I was sent to Fort Leonard Wood, Missouri, and I stayed there five or six months. It was while I was there that I met a white girl, the first white woman I had been involved intimately with. She worked at the PX and was friendly with me, so finally we went to the Service Club and had a cup of coffee and sat there and talked. She invited me to come to St. Louis where she lived. I stayed at the Jefferson Hotel, in the black neighborhood, and she came down there. I don't really think she was attractive to me because she was white. I think it was because she was the only woman available.

We got to be very close. It wasn't sex only. After I went to another camp, I'd still go up to St. Louis and see her. It went on for a while. But we never talked about marriage. I guess she's married now. Before I met her, when I had in mind that I hated all white people, I thought: *Every white woman I find I'm going to take, and I'm going to do everything to her I can do to her to make up for what they've done to us.* My intentions were not to rape them, but I knew how they felt about blacks, so I was going to use them. I changed my mind. If a woman loves you, it's not the color of her skin. It's the feeling she has for you, and the feeling you have for her. Period.

At Camp Claiborne, Louisiana, they put me in the engineering training school and I learned construction work—how to build bridges. That's where I learned how to design my home, because in the army I learned carpentry work. I was sent around to different places—Camp Polk, Louisiana, for instance. I tried to apply for as much training as I could. I wanted to go to Officers Candidate School at Fort Knox, Kentucky. But I couldn't make that.

At Fort Sill, Oklahoma, I worked as an orderly at headquarters. I became a corporal, a sergeant, then a battalion construction foreman and a sergeant-major. I used the army to make all the money I could. In the barracks I used to run crap games, and I'd cut the games. Since I was in charge of barracks, I allowed the soldiers to shoot craps if they didn't argue about my cut. If there wasn't any cut, they couldn't shoot dice. I'd cut $25 or $30 a night sometimes. I had a big box I'd put it in. I'd get the money changed to big denominations and I'd roll my money and keep it in a little tobacco sack in my shirt pocket.

I never gambled, I never drank, I never smoked. That kind of vice is too expensive, it's too destructive to the body, and I just didn't feel like I needed it. But I've done about everything a man could do to make money. Each soldier was allowed a certain amount of beer, so I used to take my beer and sell it. If the PX sold it for 30¢, I'd sell mine for half a dollar. And I used to loan money. I'd loan a guy a dollar for a dollar. He'd go off and throw it away on women and whisky, and I thought: If that's what you guys are going to do with it, I might as well get my share of it.

In 1943 I went overseas, first to Sydney, Australia, and then to Melbourne, and from Melbourne down to New Guinea. I was with the combat engineers. We slept on the ground, drank coconut juice and ate coconut for food. I was there eighteen months, and it was terrible. No one who ever lived through that kind of experience wants to remember it. In New Guinea I almost got killed, but it was a freak accident. I first hurt my left knee playing football when I was in high school. I sort of walk funny on that knee most of the time. Later I *broke* the knee and stayed in a hospital for six weeks with a cast on. In New Guinea I fell off a truck and hurt the same knee, and after that we had a raid one night and I jumped up and ran, trying to get into a foxhole, and I tripped, fell and hurt the same knee again. After all this they reclassified me, took me out of combat and put me into administrative service.

In New Guinea, there was no civilization like we know it. Just the bush people. God, I hadn't even *seen* a woman, let alone been with one. When we left there we were to go to the Philippines. We invaded Luzon, and I was right behind the invasion. That's why I have a lot of faith. I know the Lord has taken care of me, because all through that I never was scratched. I wasn't in the invasion, but I was right behind. When you were fighting Japs and you were a day behind, you were right in it. I was in headquarters helping administer first aid when I could.

We moved into Quezon City, a beautiful place with all the old Spanish buildings and customs and I began to run brothels. That's how I made my money. The fellows wanted to see the young ladies and I tried to provide them with what they wanted. It was a good business. I had my biggest house on Quezon Boulevard, with about ten girls. I had my own huts and a place downtown I rented and used for the prostitutes. The Filipinos would get the girls for me. It was a brothel, but it wasn't a filthy place. The huts were like GI tents—the kind two to four people sleep in.

My houses were integrated. Hell, I didn't care what the man was, if he was black, white, Chinese, Japanese, I wanted pesos. The going price was the equivalent of $5 in American money. If it was somebody I knew, I might give him a break. In most cases it was $5, but for lieutenants and captains we charged $10 or more. My job was to rush them and get them on their way. If a fellow'd go and stay a half an hour or more, I couldn't make any money. And those GIs, most of them, didn't worry about a whole lot of loving.

Later on for about four years in Chicago I had about 10 girls working for me. I'm ashamed of what I did then, but it did give me insights into how cruel men can be toward women. I was concerned for the girls as people, though. I suppose I wasn't all bad. I always gave the once-over to the guys who came in. If they were drunk or dirty or rambunctious, I wouldn't let them touch a girl. I always made sure the places I had were clean, had hot and cold running water, and that the sheets were changed three or four times a day.

The girls were always free to come and go. Unlike some, I never threatened a girl who left. With me, everything was a business. I don't understand how somebody would want to go to bed with a girl who's having sex with a lot of other men. I never could myself. Just to think of the risks you run, the diseases and all. But to each his own. And there are always a lot of guys who don't seem to mind. That's why I made money.

During this time in the Philippines I was going to the University of Manila business law school. You could enroll even though you hadn't finished high school. The classes were in English. They were taught by GIs and Filipinos. That's how I learned about business law and negotiable instruments and contracts. In 1944, while I was going to this school, I met a girl, Felicia. I would have married her. She was part French and Filipino—but she was white, and I couldn't bring her back to Mississippi. I loved Felicia! She was a wonderful woman. I mean she was just a beautiful woman. I was young, I didn't know anything about the kind of *care* that a woman could have for you. And Felicia was just everything that a man wanted. She looked out for me, she used to do all my shirts, she'd fix them just like I wanted them. And she was understanding. But her daddy, well, the ol' guy wasn't a racist but he just didn't care too much for me. But there wasn't any sex involved. She was a devout Catholic, and didn't believe in sex before marriage. I must have gone with Felicia for a year before I even kissed her. She was that firm. She wanted to, but she just wouldn't. Finally she broke down and kissed me, but that's as far as we ever got.

Well, finally, I asked her to marry me. She said yes and went to her father. He didn't want me to take her away from Manila. Well, my Momma and Daddy were living back in the States, so I couldn't stay over there. And I couldn't live with her in Mississippi. So it was just one helluva thing. Finally, we realized there wasn't any way possible for us to get together. And I never will forget the last time I saw her! She went down to the ship with me, and nearly killed me. We had sat up all night the night before I left. By this time we were so close that her mother and father trusted me. They let her come to my tent. And we sat there and talked and kissed all night long. The next morning we were to leave at seven. Her momma, daddy and all her little sisters and brothers came down to the dock at seven in the morning. I'll never forget how she squeezed me, crying and screaming. And she was shaking. Her mother was trying to pull her loose from me, and I was trying to hold onto her. When I got on the Landing

Ship Transport, LST458, I was sick. It took forty-two days to come back, and I vomited all the time. I couldn't eat anything. When I went over I didn't get sick. And now I'm afraid to sail, afraid I'd get seasick.

11

Alcorn College, near Fayette

When I got out of the army I went home to Decatur, and Medgar came home from France. He was getting letters from his French girlfriend, and I was getting a letter every day from Felicia. We both enrolled in Alcon College which also housed Alcorn High School. It didn't matter how old or big I was. I was going to get me at least a high school diploma, and as much college as I could get. I was a class ahead of Medgar, but we were roommates. And we lived together the whole time. We were on the GI Bill and I played football and got a scholarship, so the tuition didn't cost me anything. I'd gone in the army with nothing and I came out with about $3,000 cash, but I didn't want to spend it. I talked with the dean of men and the dean of women and asked them to let me drive a taxi, hauling people back and forth to Port Gibson for a dollar a head, and to Natchez for a dollar and a half. I bought an old car and became *the* driver for the college. We were out in the country, about seventeen miles from Port Gibson and about that far from Fayette. I got out of my high school classes around two o'clock, so I had plenty of time. We GIs were getting those GI checks and had to get them cashed, so I'd get about a thousand dollars of my money and go back to the campus and charge the other guys 50¢ for cashing their GI checks. They saved themselves 50¢ because they'd have to pay me a dollar to go in my taxi into town to cash their checks. I had them coming and going and I didn't do too bad.

I was always busy making money, but Medgar was different. He was editor of the school paper and a member of the debating team and the Glee Club. He went out for track and he played football. Plus he made good grades.

For three years I was first-string center for the Alcorn Braves. And we won the Southern Association championship for two years straight. This was an all Negro school. In those days, Southern whites and Southern blacks didn't play against each other—never. Anyway, we thought we were pretty good.

Medgar and I'd buy fresh peanuts from a farm and roast them in our room, and then every night when the teachers and kids would be hungry, just before going to bed we'd go out hollering, "Peanut man! Peanut man!"

And someone would open a window: "Come on the fourth floor."

And we'd go on up there to sell that one bag of peanuts for a dime.

Most Friday and Saturday nights all the students went to the movies. But I never could carry anyone to a movie, I didn't have time. I had to make money. I didn't want to get out of school and be walking around and having to take a teacher's job that paid about $40 a month. While all the rest went to the movies, I'd go buy some baloney and salami and cheese and peanut butter and a couple of loaves of bread and make sandwiches. When the movies was out, the grill was closed and all the kids would be hungry. So I'd go around hollering, "Sandwiches! Sandwiches! Fresh-made sandwiches!" And they'd run to the window: "Come on up!" You can fix sandwiches like that for about 5¢ and I'd sell them for 35¢.

Once we had a big football banquet, and everyone took his girlfriend. I had a friend, Frank Roosevelt, who worked in the kitchen. When the boys would take the girls out to dance, I'd motion to Frank and say, "Look, Frank, you take all of that food and put it in a box." I'd keep shoving the big baked hams down toward one end of the table and pretty soon Frank would pass by and pick it up. I kept on pushing all the food down to the end of the table, and my girlfriend nudged me: "Charles, Charles, don't do that!" And I said, "Just be quiet, be quiet."

I guess Medgar and I must have carried about thirty or forty pounds of ham to the dormitory that night—and none of it had been touched. I left my girlfriend, and said, "Look, I'll be right back." She didn't know where I was going. I carried all that meat to my room and locked it up. The banquet was over at eleven o'clock, and there were some hungry clowns. So I said, "C'mon, Medgar, let's go." We went up to our room. We had a hot table. And we left a door crack open. And as we heated the ham, we turned on a little ol' electric fan, and let it blow the smoke off the ham through the crack. And it fumed the whole building up, and those jokers were hungry, and we were hollering, "C'mon on down to Room 15! Sandwiches, $1!" And we sold over $100 worth of sandwiches.

Medgar took up business administration, and I—you wouldn't believe it—social studies. I wanted to be a lawyer.

Well, it never worked out. Neither of us got what we wanted. He went into the insurance business, and I kept hustling, doing one thing and another.

I was quite a character at Alcorn. I think it was one of those things where I'd been away a long time. I'd just been overseas too long, so when I came home I was wild. I didn't want any wife. I just wanted to have a good time. Girls came along, and if I saw someone I liked I sought after her.

Suddenly one young lady was pregnant and she said I was the father. I never denied it. And the next thing, another girl was pregnant about a month later. She accused me and I didn't deny that either. Then the third one was pregnant, and I was a father again, and I didn't deny that. Their mommas and daddies were after me, the girls were after me, and my Momma and Daddy were after me. I didn't know what to do. Anyway, I kept going to school. One was saying, "You got to marry me." And I said "I'm not going to marry a one of you!" I told them, "I'm going to go to school and finish."

The last girl that got pregnant was reported to the dean and to the president of the school. I went to the dean and tried to make a deal. I had something on him and tried to get him to let me *pretend* that I got married. Well, they sort of bought it for a while, but the chaplain wouldn't go along with it. We had a campus paper, and everytime somebody got married they printed it. I didn't want my marriage printed. I just wanted to let it be said that we got married and let the girl go on home. But they wouldn't go that route. Finally I went and got a license because they threatened to kick me out of school. I really wanted to finish school. Daddy had always said, "Look, son, try to get an education. Try at least to get a degree, whether you use it or not. Just get one." And I promised Daddy and Momma I was going to get an education, that I was at least going to get a degree. So I went and got a marriage license from the old courthouse and went back to Alcorn and told the girl I had the license. Meantime, the other two girls were away. I went down to the chaplain and said, "Marry me." He took the license and filled it out and said, "Mail it in," and I mailed it in, and that's the way we got married. We never did live together or anything. But at least I had a contract, all you need is a license. There wasn't any ceremony. She wasn't there, wasn't anyone there. Then I went and told the girl, "Okay, we're married," and that was all there was to it. We never lived together.

12

1946–47

When Medgar and I were in the army, we had been told that we were fighting for our country, so we wanted to make sure we could register and vote. We had always wanted to vote, but we had never been given that chance. In 1946 while we were at Alcorn, we went up to the county courthouse to register and they wouldn't let us come in. There was quite a commotion! Alton Graham asked, "Who you niggers think you are!"

I answered, "We've grown up here. We have fought for this country and we think we should register."

We created a scene. Graham told our daddy, "You better tell your boys if they don't want trouble they better not try to register."

Before we went to register, Medgar, the other boys and I went where Momma and Liz were washing clothes in a big tin bucket with lye soap they had made. And Momma didn't say anything. She just stood there with a stick, turning the clothes. I could see her lips moving. She was praying for us.

At first, they wouldn't let us register, but we kept after them and finally we got registered. And Graham and some of the other bigots came back to the house in Decatur to threaten Daddy: "Your boys better not come home to vote, 'cause we're gonna git 'em if they do."

On voting day ol' Bilbo was raving: "The best way to stop niggers from votin' is to visit them the night before election."

So Medgar and I said, "Well, let them come on and visit us. We are going to kill all you white folks. Just come on and visit us!"

Medgar and I recruited A. J. and C. B. Needham (A. J. Needham was my best friend and now lives in Los Angeles) and B. W. (we called him Bernon) Wansley and Hudson and went to vote. When we arrived at the courthouse, there must have been two hundred rednecks, dressed in overalls and holding their shotguns. God! You never saw so many Kluxers, bigots, racists and hatemongers. And guns! But we didn't pay them any attention. They were sitting around in their pickup trucks and standing over the courthouse square. When we tried to go into the courthouse they blocked the doors and refused to let us through. I had a long-handle .38 in my pocket and held my long switchblade in my hand. Whites are scared of blacks with knives—they hate those knives worse than guns.

We were standing on the courthouse steps, the same steps where Bilbo years before had told a white audience, "If you don't stop those two little niggers there they're gonna try to go to Washington to represent you." Then the ol' circuit clerk, Mr. Brand, came around saying, "Charles, you and Medgar, you all go back, you gonna cause trouble.

[93]

And I said, "Let me tell you something, Mr. Brand. We are going to vote, or else we're all going to go to hell. It's up to you. *Give us our ballot.*"

The clerk went back in the courthouse, and I said, "Let's split up." There are three doors going into the courthouse. "A.J., C.B., Bernon and Hudson, go in the side doors, and Medgar and I are going in the front door. Eventually we will meet at the entrance, in the clerk's office, to get our ballot." When we tried to get in the side door and the front door, they were blocked. The druggist, Andy Mays, was blocking one door, and when we tried to walk in he said, "Listen, nigger, ain't nothin' happened to you yet."

I pointed to my side pocket with the bulging .38 and flashed my switchblade knife at him and he stepped back and Medgar and I walked through. We went into the courthouse while the other boys watched to sort of protect us. We had guns.

We were inside the courthouse. We had received our ballots to vote, but there wasn't any way we could get to the ballot box, because the Klansmen had put the ballot box *inside* a back office and they were physically blocking the door to that office. I said, "Look, Medgar, I'm going through," and he replied, "No, Charley, don't try. It ain't worth it."

They stood there, and we stood there eyeballing each other. I really wanted to die that day. And again we found out they're cowards. They were shaking like leaves on a tree. There were dozens of them, big-bellied, rednecked and with guns, and scared to death.

I asked, "May I place my ballot in the ballot box?"

One said, "You niggers can't come in here."

And I replied, "Why not?"

And he said, "Cause we said so."

Andy May walked up beside me and asked, "Evers, ain't nothin' happened to you yet?"

And I answered by saying, "Isn't anything going to happen to me."

Medgar said, "Come on, Charley, we'll get them next time."

Medgar and I left. But I said to May, "Listen, we'll be back. And you better not follow us down the street."

The sheriff did not try to arrest us. We vowed we were not coming back home alive if they tried anything on us. They would have to kill us. I told Brand and the rest of them, "That's all right. One of these days you're going to want to come in the door and we ain't going to let you in."

May said, "You niggers better get away from here before somethin' happens!"

I replied, "Ain't nothin' going to happen to us, except what happens to you, too."

Then Medgar and I called the others and we left. Blacks who worked in cafés were peeking out from the windows, others were looking from behind posts. They thought sure the whites were going to kill us. After we'd gone about a mile, a couple of whites drove alongside of us in their car, threatening, "We gonna take care of you niggers tonight!"

I said, "If you weren't a coward, you'd get out of the car and take care of us right now!"

But they didn't. They just sped off.

Another car came along and slowed down. They taunted us, so I pulled out my .38 and said, "You see that! I'll blow your brains out if you get out of that car!" They sped off, like the others.

A. J. and C. B. Needham cut through the white school campus, and the other boys left. Medgar and I went down the street. A group of white cowards started following us, cussing us and threatening us: "We'll git you tonight, niggers!"

"All right, crackers, we are going to get you now," we told them. "Come on down here—*now*."

They turned around and went back.

We were the first ones to vote. We voted in the next county election. That was in 1947. By the way they guarded that ballot box, they let us know there was something mighty good in voting. They didn't want us to start voting—not even in a town where the white folks had us outnumbered.

Every summer while Medgar and I were attending Alcorn, we'd go to Chicago to get jobs. We'd work in meatpacking plants or do anything we could. We had a raggedy car, and we'd drive all the way, taking turns at the wheel. When we would stop at service stations for gas or oil, the white man wouldn't let us use the washroom, so we would have to go down in the woods along the roadside, trying to hide ourselves while the cars were passing.

I was still going to Alcorn when the army called me back and sent me to Fort Hood, Texas. I was there when I got a telegram from Eva and Liz that our baby sister, Mary Ruth, was dying. I drove straight through; and when I walked in the room she hugged and kissed me. Soon after that she was dead. She was only twenty-one.

After I came out of service the second time, my wife Nan went to live with Momma and I went back to school. I lacked a few hours, not quite a semester, so I finished the semester and got my degree. When we moved to Philadelphia, Mississippi, in 1951 I got a job teaching history and coaching football at a little town just north of Philadelphia called Noxapater. It paid $100 a month. I wanted to put our daughter Pat in the Noxapater school because I didn't want her going to the run-down school in Philadelphia. I wanted to send her to school where I knew it was best. I said, "If I'm going to teach in Noxapater, my daughter's certainly going to school where I'm teaching."

I carried her there, but the Negro principal—an *Uncle Tom*—had me arrested. They said it was the wrong district and I couldn't do it, and they put me in jail. It was my first arrest. It was a regular ol' calaboose, not much bigger than a telephone booth, right down on the ground; white folks were passing and cussing me, and I'd waggle my finger at them. Pat, who was in the third grade, was crying. And I said, "Don't worry, baby, Daddy will be back. And I'll be going to more jails before I'm through."

The year I went to live in Philadelphia, Medgar was a senior at Alcorn. When he finished, he moved to Mound Bayou, an all-Negro community, to sell hospitalization and life insurance and burial insurance. The burial-insurance business was owned by our uncle, Mark Thomas, who also had started a funeral parlor in Philadelphia. I took over the funeral parlor and lived upstairs. At this time, my Daddy had gotten sick and there was no hospital in Decatur, so he had to go to Union, between Decatur and Philadelphia. We rushed him to the hospital and they put him in the basement, where water was running and there were roaches and rats. I raised all kinds of hell about it, but there wasn't anything I could do. This was in 1953. I tried to insist that they put him in a ward, but they refused. When he died they called me and I jumped in the ambulance to go after him. Being an undertaker I knew how bodies were handled, and I didn't want my daddy handled that way. So I went and got him. And the white doctor said, "How in hell can you do something like that? If you can pick up your own dead daddy and drive him back to Philadelphia, then you ain't got no kind of heart."

And I replied, "You've got enough heart to put him down in a place like this and let him die. Sure I've got enough heart to carry him in my own ambulance. I'd rather do it than see some of you do it."

Then I rolled Daddy on out and put him in the ambulance. When I got back to Philadelphia I was going to embalm him, but those around me wouldn't let me do that. But I looked on there while they embalmed him. And I dressed him myself. Then I went upstairs, and it was strange knowing that my Daddy was downstairs, dead, and me upstairs, trying to sleep. But I couldn't sleep.

At church, for the funeral, I broke down, and passed out. First I'd seen Eddie die. Then Ruth. And now Daddy. I didn't know then that I would lose my mother before too long . . . and Medgar would be shot.

In Philadelphia I started a campaign to register blacks. I was elected voter-registration chairman for the Negroes of Mississippi. I pushed Medgar to become the first Negro to enroll at Ole Miss, and he wrote Alcorn asking that his records be sent to the University of Mississippi's School of Law. Early in 1954 the *Jackson Daily News* ran the headline NEGRO APPLIES TO ENTER OLE MISS. Myrlie, Medgar's wife, feared for his life, but he said, "You have to make sacrifices to make progress."

Myrlie was an attractive woman, but she and I have never been that close. I think I resented her because I never wanted Medgar to get married. I wanted there to be just the two of us brothers alone against the world.

Eight months after Medgar applied, Attorney General Coleman asked him if he would accept an out-of-state scholarship. Medgar refused and told him, "I plan to live on campus in a dormitory, to use the library, eat in the dining hall, attend classes. But let me assure you that I bathe regularly, that I wear clean clothes and that none of the brown of my skin will rub off. I won't contaminate the dormitory or the food."

Soon after that the Board of Higher Learning announced that Medgar's application to Ole Miss was rejected. His application was kept on file so that a suit could be started at any time. I urged Medgar to go for the job of state field secretary of the NAACP rather than pursue the case in court. And he did—and he got the job.

Meanwhile, I was working at four or five different jobs. I had the funeral parlor and burial insurance. And I asked Negroes in Philadelphia if they had ever heard of a colored cab, and they said, "Ah, man, they won't let you have no colored cabs in Philadelphia." Remember, this is Philadelphia, Miss., not Philadelphia, Pa. And I said, "I'm going to try." I started driving, but the white drivers said, "You can't go to the bus station and pick up passengers." And I said, "Why not? Are you big enough to stop me?"

I bought another car and hired someone else to drive. I already had a hotel with a downstairs café. That café gave colored people the first chance they ever had to go to a place and get milkshakes—and sit down. They could order them at a takeout stand at a white drugstore, but they couldn't sit down. I fixed it so they could get milkshakes, sodas and other things and sit down like anybody else. The cab business was going good. After the whites found out that I was determined to operate and was legally operating, they didn't bother me too often. I was the first Negro to start a cab company.

I was also the first Negro disc jockey in Mississippi. I was on station WOKJ and had a very good listening response. Negroes patronized the businesses that I was advertising. I would always say, "Pay your poll tax. Register and vote." I'd say this when I came on the air and when I'd go off the air. And I'd tell them, "If you can't register to vote, pay your poll tax anyway." The white racists and bigots didn't like that, so I was a problem. The White Citizens Council—that's the Klan without sheets—was tampering me about this, and tampered the people who owned the station, people by the name of Coles.

I was beginning to make good money, even had a bank account. White folks there couldn't stand to see a black man making it. They didn't think about my working fifteen and sixteen hours a day and holding down three or four jobs. They didn't care about that. In their minds a black man wasn't supposed to make money, to get ahead. They didn't like my being state chairman of voter registration and Medgar's being head of the NAACP—two weapons they knew would destroy racism and destroy their power over us.

The racists flat broke me. But before they did, they tried to hire a black man to kill me. A white man (who soon became mayor of that town) called me and said, "Charles, there's going to be a Negro who's going to come to your house and ask you to drive him to the county line, where the Kluxers are going to kill you." He warned me that the rednecks had paid him off to get out where they could knock me off. Soon this black man came and rang my bell. I acted as if I didn't know anything. "C'mon," he said, "I want you to carry me down to the county line."

"Well, isn't Obiedow"—he's the guy who drove for me— "around there someplace?"

"But I want you to carry me. I need to talk with you about somethin'."

"I'm going to stay in," I said.

"C'mon, c'mon, I'll give you $5."

All the time I had my .38 in my pocket. "You're going to tempt me," I said. "C'mon in." When he came in I struck him. "You dirty sonofabitch, you!" I grabbed a sawed-off baseball bat I kept handy and beat him down. My wife started screaming and I said, "I should kill this sonofabitch." Then I said, "Get this bastard out before I kill him."

Then they got to the men who owned the building my restaurant was in and pressured him into refusing to extend my lease. Next was the cab stand. They fixed it so I couldn't get my license renewed. Then they harassed the man I bought caskets from. It had to be on a cash-and-carry basis or no casket. Finally, they refused to sell me caskets. Then they began to create incidents—running into my hearse and cabs. Then they would sue me. They finally broke me. They wanted to take me off the radio station. They told Mr. Coles, "He's talking too much about voting and paying your poll tax. We don't want these niggers voting!" And they threatened to take away all the advertising spots if he didn't let me go. I went myself, because I didn't want to see him put out of business.

The racists sued us three or four times; the last suit was for $5,000 and I didn't have the money to pay it. Then they went to court and got a judgment against us and took everything we had—they wanted to take my car, but I hadn't paid for it, so they couldn't take it—and attached all my property.

When they came into our home in Philadelphia and took our furniture and things to auction it off—that was really sad. I'd just bought my wife a $400 dining-room suite for Christmas and they took it out and auctioned it for $100. We didn't have money to leave Philadelphia, so the people went around and took up a collection. They gave me $26 in pennies and dimes. I sent my wife and children down to her mother's and got in my car and headed for Flint, Michigan, to get a job. I didn't have enough money to get further than Chicago. So I stayed there with my sister. This was in 1956.

13

Chicago, 1956–63

Man, it was rough in Chicago. We bought day-old bread
and neck bones, 50¢ worth at a time. We lived in a basement with the roaches, water dripping through the pipes.
We'd go to bed and the rats were there with us.

I found a job at the packing house, carrying meat, and
made about $60 a week, working from eight to four. I had
a friend who knew somebody that worked at a hotel,
so I got an evening job from six to twelve as washroom
attendant for about $3 a night plus part of the tips. During
conventions, the rednecks from Mississippi and Georgia
and Alabama would come. And every time I'd get a half
a chance I'd do something ugly to them. For example, if
one staggered in drunk I'd take his pocketbook and take
every penny out of it and put it back in his suit and get
him out of the washroom. And another one would come
in and drop his money and I'd put my foot on it. Oh, I'd

make from $50 to $100 on such nights. All the tips, plus my salary. I kept whisky on hand, too. Some old drunk would come in: "Hey, boy! Where can I get a half pint?" I'd get $5 for it.

I never did get black women for white men. I couldn't do that. It was a very personal thing. Not because I was against white men with black women or white women with black men, but because I knew the price we'd paid in Mississippi—if a black man looked at a white woman he was lynched. And I was going to make sure I didn't help any white man get to a black woman. The white men would say, "You wanna make $10?"

"Doin' what?"

"Go git me a colored girl and bring her to my room."

"Now, you got the wrong man. I don't do anything like that."

"How the hell you make money?"

"Just like I'm doin', brushin' you down."

While I had that job I met a friend who had a bar and needed some help. I didn't know anything about a bar at that time, but I began working there on weekends for $5 a night, and I saved every penny of it. Somehow the Lord took care of me. I just kept going for three long years. I didn't do anything but work and go to church on Sunday.

I turned to policy. I started out as a runner. I was dropping policy, picking up policy—a field runner. As I learned the game, I began to drop my own policy, on the same route, under the same protection. I started off with a bankroll of $500. The first night I let them hit, for $100, but I'd taken in about $300. Then the next night I didn't let anybody hit. I took it all in, and that's how I got started. When you take in all the money for about a week, you got enough money to operate, if you don't let somebody catch you. But with a new wheel, you gotta let them catch once in a while, and I'd let them catch a small amount.

Policy, at least the way I did it, was a system of matching numbers. I don't want to get any of my old colleagues into trouble, and I'm only speaking for my game, but it was rigged from beginning to end. You'd have your runners out picking up numbers from customers, then you'd put them into a bowl.

By this time, though, the drawing has already been taken care of. The big bettors who could break you were already out of the running. And you'd sort out some little guy to win. You could tell by the address and the amount he bet.

Fortunately, nobody had the right to look at the numbers in that bowl. Ever. Most people just played from their apartments and never saw the operation at all.

When you did let people win, it was strictly for advertising purposes, so they'd spread the word. You'd want the word to get out, so people'd say, "I caught Evers for $100." At times, when you were really way ahead, you'd let somebody catch $2000 or $3000. And then business would boom.

It's up to the fellow who spins the wheel—I know it was up to us—to let you win or not. A large percentage of blacks in the ghettoes play policy—maybe as high as 90 percent. A small operator, if he has any sense, lets somebody win most days. But in general the players lose.

Mine was a small operation. I was my own runner. I was operating under the pretense of running for a big wheel. The police never really knew I was on my own. And the guys I worked for were so big they didn't know it, either. I wasn't greedy. If I could make $400 or $500 a week, I was satisfied. And believe it or not, I was never taken down to the station house. I was stopped a few times, but I kept the police paid off and never had to worry.

The big wheel was owned by both black and white. This one happened to be owned by a white, managed and run by blacks. So that's how we were able to get in there. The Mafia had control of the big numbers. They'd run the Jones boys out of Chicago down to Mexico and had taken over. And most of us in the numbers racket were operating for or under the whites. And that's why I didn't mind taking the money. I'd take every dime I could get. As a runner you make your round and pick up the policy and drop it. You're responsible for your station, and once you've turned your money you've cleared. That's all that matters.

There's nothing friendly or casual about the numbers racket. Oh no! It's rough and it's enforced. And you got to do exactly what you're told or else you don't have a job—and maybe a life—if they catch you messing up. It's as simple as that. And once you get in it, you're in it, and no getting out of it. In my case, I guess I'm one of the lucky ones who was crazy enough to try it. I always felt like I shouldn't overplay my hand. I had done well for about three or four years, and that was all I needed. They got a new police commissioner, O. W. Wilson, from California, and he was rough, and I got out.

I bought me a building after that and opened a liquor store and tavern. Then I went in the jukebox business. Some people weren't too happy about that. The syndicate told me I couldn't own jukeboxes. But I stood firm and told them, "You put one in here. We'll bust it apart." No sir, the whites are not going to have jukeboxes in my places. I don't care who the man says he is or represents, he's not going to come in my place and put in his jukeboxes. It's my place and my people. And they're going to play my jukeboxes.

I had three taverns: one on the South Side (called Club Mississippi), one on the West Side (Subway Lounge) and another in Argo (The Palm Gardens). Besides my bars I had a good bootlegging business. After two in the morning you couldn't sell—not legally. And before twelve on Sundays you couldn't sell. And that's when my business was good. I had what I called The Club House. When all the other joints closed we moved down to this hideout, where the drinks cost more because we had to pay the police off.

In the meantime I was teaching school. Can you imagine me running policy and teaching school? I was teaching physical education and history. And I was a good teacher. All the kids loved me. I taught at Robbins, Illinois, just out of Chicago, an all-black town. They were eighth-grade kids. I was making $3,800 a year.

Most of my ambition came from Conrad Hilton. I saw the man when I worked as a washroom attendant at the Palmer House in Chicago. He'd come there once in a while for meetings of hotel men, and he'd give a talk. And all of us heard him. I was a greenhorn, but I know one thing he said that stuck with me: "Own everything you can, and run nothing." He said *everybody* loves to be in business. You can always find somebody you can put in business and you'll come out on top because you'll be the one that will really get the profit. He even concessioned out the shoeshine stand. Everything in his business he had a concession on. We were sitting there listening along with the hotel managers and the big shots. A lot of people don't know how I run my business. I concession everything I got out—my liquor store, my grocery store, the restaurant. I get a flat salary for all three. I own them, but I don't really run them.

And another thing, you don't get business mixed up with civil rights. You can't spend civil rights. You can spend business. The reason I was able to do anything was because I was never dependent upon white folks. The Lord saw to it that I got to be independent of white people. I depended upon *my* people for a living. Now I can work and fight with them, and I can work and fight *for* them, without any economic reprisals being brought against me.

14

June 1963

I was operating clean. I still had the tavern business in
Chicago, and I had a building I'd bought at Sixty-Second
and Normal for Medgar and me. This building was income for us. It had 24 units and I lived on the first floor.
The Sunday before the Tuesday that Medgar was killed,
he called me from Mississippi. Medgar and I always felt it
was going to be me. And we promised each other that if
anything ever happened to one of us, the other would
carry on. Medgar telephoned and said, "Charley, be careful. 'Cause it's worse there than it is here."

I replied, "No, you're the one to be careful. Because you
know those Kluxers down there are after you. And if they
can stop you, they'll feel like they've got everything under
control."

"Don't worry about me," he said, "I'm going to make it.
You just be careful."

Somehow we both wound up crying over the phone. Then I asked, "Look, you want me to come home?"

"No, you're due to come anyway next week."

We had planned to go to South America. We had bought some land there and I'd just bought a brand-new Cadillac, black, with all the trimmings, because Medgar and I were going to see the land we'd bought down in Brazil, about fifty miles north of Brasilia. We'd planned to go down there and relax for a month. Then we were going to drive back to Chicago for the NAACP convention. We were talking about this trip over the phone and Medgar said, "Be careful now. I'll see you in a week."

That was Sunday night. Then it must have been about 3 A.M. Wednesday morning—I drove in front of my building and saw all the lights, and I reached for my gun —I always carried a gun while in Chicago. Before getting out of the car I looked around to see if I could spot anybody. I thought about Pat, my daughter, because she used to get sick. I jumped out of the car and could see shadows of heads through a window, and I knew something was wrong. I'd closed my business for the night, and I had my money sack in one hand and my gun in the other. I ran to the porch and someone opened the door. The room was filled with people, and everyone was looking at me real solid. There must've been a dozen people there, and I said, "What's wrong? Where's Pat?" And someone said, "She's asleep." My wife Nan came and said softly, "Come on back here, Charles." And she motioned me to a back room.

"What's wrong?" I said. "Something happen to Medgar?" By then I just knew it.

"Yes. They shot him."

"Aw, well, they probably just winged him. They can't kill the Evers boys. They've been trying too long."

"No, Charles, he's dead."

And that's all I remember. Nan said later that I told her, "Pack my things." They took me and put me on an airplane. I didn't come to my senses until I was in Jackson and got off the plane. Nan said I told her, "I'll never come back to Chicago. I ain't comin' back. I shouldn't have left Mississippi in the first place." I left everything I had.

God, how I hated every white man! And how I hated Charles Evers. Because if I had been with Medgar, Beckwith never would have killed him. I always go prepared. But Medgar didn't carry a gun. I felt that if I'd stayed in Mississippi, Medgar wouldn't be gone. All the way back to Mississippi I thought of the times when we were boys and we'd say, "When we get to be men, we're going to do something for our people." We started when we were just boys, just the two of us. And now that he was gone, I had nobody. I prayed to God that I wouldn't break down. Medgar wouldn't want me to break down. He was tough like that. We both used to pretend just how tough we could be. We'd always say, "It shows weakness when you cry. Medgar used to say, "Don't hate 'em, Charley. Don't hate 'em." But, God, I hated. I hated. . . .

I often wonder what I'd do if I saw Beckwith again. A while ago, I'd have broken his neck. I think today I'd just look at him and pity him. I always remember Governor Ross Barnett going up to him in court and shaking his hand. I think Beckwith was in the fertilizer business. Maybe still is.

It was such a crime. Medgar was such a good guy. To lay down in front of a man's house and shoot him as he was coming out of his front door. Everybody knew about his work. He wasn't flamboyant or anything. By coincidence, the night that Medgar died the President had just said something about doing away with racial killings.

I held up pretty good in Mississippi. I came to myself after I got there. I'll never forget Dan Rather of CBS.

He stayed around at the funeral home and consoled me. He went with me to the morgue because I'd asked about Medgar's hair. Medgar and I always wore our hair in the same style, and I'd asked Myrlie, Medgar's wife, about his hair, and she said she thought he needed a haircut. We'd always worn what we called a low English, and I still wear it. It's not long and it's not short, just medium. I wanted his hair cut like that. So I went down and carried the barber with me. And when I went to the morgue, I still couldn't believe it was really true. It was the first time I'd seen him since he was shot.

We had the funeral in Jackson, and again I held up pretty good. Sure I gave a little, but I didn't really break down. We loaded him on a train to take him to Washington, and in Washington we brought his body to Reverend E. Franklin Jackson's church. And afterward, when we started out the church door and I saw the casket being carried out, I thought: *Well, Senator Bilbo, looks like we're here.* And I just went to pieces. I couldn't take it. They finally carried me off someplace. Bobby Kennedy tried to console me. Then we went on out to Arlington Cemetery. Bobby stayed right with me during the service. I'll never forget that. And then we went to the White House. I was there with Medgar's family. My family stayed in Jackson. But Myrlie and her children and I went to the White House, and we stayed there with the President the rest of the day.

It was at Medgar's funeral that I met Dr. Martin Luther King for the first time. I'll never forget him. He came in shirtsleeves. I admired this because I always liked to be different myself. Everybody else was hot and perspiring, but Martin stayed cool. I went up and introduced myself to him. We became close friends.

After that, whenever he had a march and needed help, I'd go get him some bodies. And he'd do the same for me.

We'd do anything for each other. Can you imagine anything sillier than somebody starting a rumor that Martin liked women? Now, if he had a hankering for men, that's something else. That's my argument with J. Edgar Hoover. I mean, who's talking about whom? I'd say this to Hoover: You don't have any women anywhere. We might go and check *you* out.

After the funeral I went back to Mississippi. I haven't thought of living anyplace else since. I was born here, and I'll die here.

15

1963

In Jackson, the day before Medgar's funeral, some of the
black people were looking for someone to take Medgar's
place, and I said, "Look, you don't have to look any further.
Because I'm going to take his place." The NAACP people
in New York didn't like that very much. They didn't
know how much they could control me. It is not a secret
that Roy Wilkins and I have not been able to communi-
cate. Roy was shaving when he heard over the radio
that I was taking Medgar's job, and a friend told me that
Roy said, "I almost slit my throat." He thought he should
be the one to decide.

Before Medgar was buried I guess they figured it
wouldn't look good to say I couldn't have it. They knew I
was going to take it anyway. I didn't care about any title. I
was just going to do what he was doing. They finally let
me become the field secretary, so I moved into Medgar's

old office on Lynch Street in Jackson and started working.

Secretly, I wanted to do what he and I had planned to do a long time ago. That was to organize a Mau Mau gang to kill two whites for every black they killed. I was going to do it by myself. I planned to sort of float around in Mississippi and kill a white man once a week, in a different part of the state. I was going to do it different each time. I was going to poison some, stab some and shoot some. Just killing the man who killed Medgar wouldn't have been enough for me. I saw him once, in a courtroom. I felt the only way to stop the white man was to kill him. And I was going to take my time—wasn't going to be in any hurry. I was going to kill one big white racist in every county.

I secured some equipment, several guns, and I looked around. But something kept telling me, "That's not the way, Charles, that's not the way." This battle was going on within myself. Every day I'd go to the office and sit at Medgar's desk; it was like he was there with me, and something kept saying, "Medgar wouldn't want it like that. That's not the way, that's not the way." I began to get busy. Gradually I got away from the idea of killing white people physically. I decided I could kill them better by doing what Medgar had been doing. And that's when I got busy getting people registered. I think I tried to get killed. I really wanted them to kill me. I'd take a few people with me, and I challenged and provoked all the white racist cops and sheriffs and highway patrol all over Mississippi. I did everything to make them kill me. I guess I was stupid, but I felt only one way. I told my people: "Stand up to them. If they aren't hiding under sheets or don't have you outnumbered, they're scared to death. They won't do anything unless you turn your back."

Black people all over the state worshiped Medgar, and they wanted to protect me because of him. They offered to stand beside me, to drive a car for me. But I'd drive, I'd go

[114]

by myself. I felt that if I had to go, I'd go the same way Medgar did. I mean it, even today. I know that sounds real stupid—and I don't have any death-wish. Basically, I want to live on. I want to accomplish something in my life. Medgar pushed and pushed until he really accomplished something. I, too, after my death want my life to be meaningful.

I've always known and understood the difference between Medgar and me. I've always seemed more militant, but I wasn't more militant than Medgar. I was what you'd call more vocal, "sassy." I'd talk big, cuss people out. Medgar was more forceful. He would plan and wait. Medgar was real quiet and he didn't talk about what he was going to do, but he'd do things. He was very level-headed, always in the background. He planned everything, but stayed in the background. He would put someone else in the foreground, except when it came to a difficult situation, then Medgar would come to the front. I'd say, "We got to start using guns, shoot some of them." Medgar's reply was, "No, Charley, we'll get them other ways." That's the way he was. As for me, I'd be steamed up and want to take you on right now. I'd say, "Don't wait around, let's get it over right now."

Medgar's death made one point clear to me. I had to change Mississippi not by shouting at people, but by giving blacks the courage to get registered and start voting. I followed in Medgar's footsteps. Aaron Henry and I worked as a team through Mississippi. We helped develop the community, that's why the NAACP is so strong in Mississippi. We have strong leaders in most of our chapters. The elected black officials in public office are NAACP presidents or board members who have been active in our branches. That's how they were elected to public office, through the organization.

We go into areas that are still ruled by racists who keep

black people frightened and silent. We try to insist that people become aware of their surroundings and find a potential leader. Once the philosophy is planted, we move on to another place to organize, promote and work to get people registered. You can see how strong Port Gibson, Natchez, Woodville and Hazlehurst are. These are local branches. In Indianaol and Sunflower county, you have strong chapters.

Attitudes are changing. It's all because we didn't lose our heads. When Medgar was killed, if I'd started teaching hate and denouncing the white folks and blaming the black folks, where would this state be? I know my attitude has helped to change things because I'm the one they hear from the most. That's why I tell my black brothers to say the right thing.

Roy Wilkins was asked when the NAACP was going to get militant and he said it's always been militant. It's a matter of priorities. When we started, if we'd screamed "Black Power" we'd have been lynched. So we set our priorities: getting the vote and doing away with lynching. This has made it possible for us to speak out as we do today. The NAACP is responsible for the anti-lynching law and the Supreme Court decision to desegregate the schools. Some folks criticize the NAACP. Let me tell you something: The NAACP has been the most forceful, the most achieving organization in the whole history of our race. Had it not been for the NAACP that Medgar started in Mississippi, we would not be here doing what we're doing now.

Medgar, Aaron Henry and I worked to build the NAACP from one branch to the largest number of local branches of any state in the South, and the largest membership. Out of all who started out when we opened the NAACP offices in 1954 in Jackson, Aaron and I are the only ones still around. Everyone else has been shot, bombed to death or run out of the state. The NAACP has been everything to black people in Mississippi. It has been the mother, the father, the counselor, the vehicle any community should have. Women would come to us and ask assistance on their husband's weekly earnings. They would come to us about their children being sick and they couldn't get them in a hospital. We would always help them. Someone would die in the family and they didn't have anyone to help them with the funeral arrangements. We were available twenty-four hours a day. We would get up at one or two in the morning and drive 150 or 200 miles to see about somebody. Medgar did it, Aaron did it, and I did it.

16

The blacks had just organized an NAACP chapter in Shreveport, Louisiana, and asked me to come over and help them get started. When they announced over radio and TV that I was coming, all hell broke loose. The whites treated it like the devil himself was coming in to rabblerouse all their "good niggers." Reverend Allen Johnson of Jackson, Mississippi, said, "I'm going with you, Charles," so we drove down Highway 80 toward Louisiana, and we kept seeing those Klan signs along the road. We were used to seeing them painted on state highways, but every mile we would see a sign. We arrived at Monroe and headed toward Shreveport. Just before we got to Shreveport we stopped for gas and a black man working at the station sneaked around and whispered that the Klan was out in force waiting for me. He said the Klan had been bragging that I would not get out of Louisiana alive. But he sort of laughed, "They won't be expecting you in a Cadillac!"

When we got to the bridge going into Shreveport, there must have been five hundred Kluxers, all over the road.

I said, "Oh hell, they have us."

Reverend Johnson said, "Don't worry, I'm going to pray."

I said, "Pray, hell. It won't stand any praying, they are going to get us this time."

"Don't worry, I'm going to pray. And you just keep driving."

I kept driving. They were peeking and peering at all the broken-down cars. They didn't recognize us and we went right on through. When we got over the bridge, into Shreveport, we drove to the Baptist church where I was supposed to speak, and it was packed with folks from all around, and police were circling, flashing their red beacon lights.

I started on my speech. The church had loudspeakers, so for the benefit of the cops that were circling the church I said, "You dirty bigots. One day the shoe's going to be on the other foot." After I had completed about half of my speech, one red-necked sheriff yelled out to me, "Hey, you, *boy*, you ain't gonna speak here," and they tried to run me off the platform, but I said, "I ain't going any-place."

In the meantime, the police were beating the people on the outside, forcing them into the church—driving and beating them like they were a herd of cattle. I saw a young black man run down from the choir and the police knocked him down right in the aisle and beat him back up to the pulpit. I was still standing there in the pulpit and Reverend Johnson said, "Come on, Charles, get out of here." He pulled me on out the back door and forced me into the car. Someone shouted, "They're waiting for you at the bridge. Charles, they're going to kill you."

I said, "Aw, hell, they ain't going to kill anybody."

Reverend Johnson said, "Charles, you're not going back across that bridge. We got to get you out some kind of way, because all they want is you. They don't want me. I'm going to take this car back home. I'll fool them, because they'll think you're in the car. And this will give you time to get away."

Reverend Johnson got into the car. Sure enough, he drove all through those Kluxers, and they trailed him, waiting until he was on an isolated road. Meanwhile, my other friends had taken me over to the house of the secretary of the NAACP branch and they hid me in the basement. The cops figured I was over there, but they didn't find me.

Later, we decided to march on Alcorn because the president was working black teachers for $70 per month. It was my alma mater and I didn't feel that my school should be treating its teachers so bad. We tried to talk with him but he wouldn't listen. We started our protest and we got the blacks involved. The rednecks were ready for us—they had about five hundred bloodthirsty highway patrolmen, state troopers and national guardsmen. We marched to the campus and they blocked us. I was in front,—and there were about two thousand people behind me.

"You ain't nothin' but murderers," I said. "You ain't got the guts to shoot me. You are sitting there with that gun in your hand, shaking. You ain't got the guts nor the courage to pull the trigger. If we turn our backs you'll shoot all of us down." Then I told them, "I've just a good mind to walk right over you. What would you do? Would you shoot me?" I remember the little trooper standing there, just shaking. He was paralyzed. We moved in on them, and they started beating us with their clubs. Reverend Johnson pushed me back, saying "Now, listen, Charles, you stay back, let me go. They'll kill you. They'll just beat me." You don't find many folks like that, he didn't just *say* it, he went. They beat him down, and I couldn't get to him because they were holding me back. That's the kind of man you can't forget.

Thank God the racists can't kill all of us who believe in freedom. Reverend R. L. T. Smith, in Jackson, has been one of the long-time stalwarts. He's been like a father to me. He has been my adviser, has been with me on marches and in jail, and he has been with me when we were teargassed two or three times. Reverend Smith was the president of our Jackson movement and helped lead the boycott in Jackson. His store and his house were blasted a number of times, but he never gave up. He's one of the few preachers who's worth something. Reverend Smith carries a gun and wouldn't hesitate to use it. He would pray and shoot—or, more likely, shoot and then pray. Most preachers say things, but when it comes to proving it, most of them don't. It has been a whole lot of people who have helped to make our freedom movement. Dozens of Negroes that we know of have been killed by racists and most of those that have done the killing are known—like the ones who killed the three civil rights workers. They picked them up in Philadelphia, Miss. They found out *who* they were, *what* they had done and *how* they had done it. They had a trial and sentenced them. If justice is to be done it may be because two of the boys killed were white.

I'll never forget Andrew Goodman. Aaron Henry and I sent him over to Meridian to join the other civil rights workers. He hardly stopped. He got to Jackson and was there about thirty minutes, then he was sent on to Philadelphia with Michael Schwerner and James Chaney. We never saw them alive again. James Chaney was black and a native of Mississippi, and Schwerner and Goodman were white and from New York. Their bodies were so well hidden it took federal officials more than a month to uncover them. Everyone knew that their lynching was a Klan conspiracy. This happened in June 1964. This same year, on one evening, the Klan burned between eighty and ninety crosses throughout the state. They left some of their literature around. Besides the blacks, the Klan's enemies include Jews, Catholics, Orientals, revolutionists, socialists—and "foreign elements."

In 1964 more than a thousand young white boys and girls came down to Mississippi to work for civil rights, and they lived and worked with Negro families. That's when things started to change in Mississippi. They came down and saw how the system really worked. How the bigots and racists oppressed the black person, and how they would attack a white person and beat his head if he was helping Negroes. The young students who came to Mississippi in 1964 got a taste of the racist's hatred, and they vowed they were going to do something about it. They saw how we were treated. They told their friends back home, and they talked about integration. The young people are the future of this country, the black and the white. The kind of attitudes and the kind of things they do will determine where we go in the future. If they're going to become the hate-mongers and the extremists, then our country's going to be hate-monger and extremist.

I ask again and again of white folks: Do you know why people rebel? It's because no one will listen to them. The same with the young people in the colleges, if the administration would listen to them they'd solve a lot of problems. And we're going to be with our young folks in Mississippi. You see, young people are no different from old folk. If you got something sound and sensible, they'll listen and be a part of it. But the young—like the Negro—has been shut up, and we've got to be heard or we're going to tear the door down. That's all there is to it. And you'd do the same thing, no matter who you are.

To the young blacks of Mississippi, I say: Go and tell your mommas and daddies to stand up to the whites. Tell them that you don't want to go to Chicago when you get grown. You don't want to go to New York to get a job. You want to stay in Mississippi. This is your home. You stay here in Mississippi, build homes and factories here. Be a part of it. You don't want to go up there and find a job. This is your country here. And let these whites know that you can be mayor, you can be sheriff, you can be on the school board, if you just care enough.

As for those who have left, I say come back home. You can do more for yourself and your people here than you could in 100 years up there. Opportunities are opening up. There's plenty of wide open space. The air is better. The pollution is less. Nobody's afraid of whites mobbing or lynching. In fact, we're having a reverse migration to the South in general.

The grown-up blacks will have to get behind the local youth and support them. We have to get out there and follow them, do what they ask us to do—as long as they're right. We have to let black people know there isn't anybody in the world greater than we are. We are more affectionate. We have to let white folks know that all the hate they've built against us is now being turned back on them. White folks taught us to hate. Hate's turning around. The white folks can't understand why their sons are rising against them and saying the system is no good. Why daughter is disobeying mother, why nephews are shooting uncles, why the white sons are saying, "Momma, you're nothing" and "Daddy, you're nothing." White parents can't understand why their children turn into beatniks, hippies and yippies and others. It's the American system that has caused this resentment. It has provoked the young kids into rebelling. They're only fulfilling the Bible: *The son shall rise against the father and the daughter against the mother.* Children look parents in the eye and say, "No, we're not going to have it. You're wrong. You mistreated black folks and the poor Indian. You annihilated the Indians. You took their land. Ah, you're wrong." God's going to work on it. And we're going to keep pushing. But let's not lose our head. The fact is that the American system is now beginning to bring in some blacks, their voices are being heard. Many whites are beginning to listen. This shows some progress. I don't know how much, but it's showing some. Maybe student unrest was caused because the adults wanted only comfort, the status quo, and the answer to student unrest might be more adult unrest.

I was talking to a group of students at one of those exclusive private schools in the East where rich white folks send their children. And one of the young men—he was from New Orleans—said that since he'd come East he'd met many intelligent Negroes, and he asked me, "How can I ever prove to my parents that what they taught me about blacks is all wrong?"

Son, now that you know the difference, you've got to go back and convince Momma and Daddy that they've got to give the black people who live in New Orleans a chance. This has never happened. You've got to expose Momma and Daddy to one of your black friends. You've got to take a black friend home with you and tell them, Momma and Daddy, you've got to talk to one of my black friends. I want you to know that they're not what you taught us. What you've taught us has been wrong. You might think they'll get angry. But you're their son, and there's only so much they're going to do to their own son, or their own daughter. If you go to Sunday school or church, you should tell the white racists there—and there's plenty of them in the churches, they're the most segregated places in America—you should tell them what they don't know: That we're just God's children, we're no different. That all we need is a chance.

What white Americans have been saying about us is wrong. If we're poor, if we're ignorant, we're no different from white people who never had a chance. Go to Virginia and to Kentucky. The poor whites there are just as backward and just as ignorant as many blacks. It's the same with the Mexicans and the Indians. So go carry that message to Momma and Daddy. And tell them and others to *open that door* and give us a chance. Whatever your mommas and daddies have been, son, don't blame them. They've been taught that 'white is right' and 'black is wrong'—and they're afraid. Most people are afraid of change, even when it's for the good. You've got to work on them by telling them the truth.

Whites must understand why black people are beginning to hate. My God! Who has given us a reason not to hate? There's only one issue: Just be fair. Whatever we are, our white brothers made us.

17

I'll never forget the first time I went to Washington after Medgar's death to see President Kennedy. This was in 1963. We had a meeting of all the black leaders from all over the country, and President Kennedy came in and spoke to us, briefly. He was in a hurry and went right on out. And Louis Martin, the Negro who was in charge of minority groups for the Democrats, came in. We told Louis how difficult it was trying to register and vote in Mississippi. We asked for assistance. There must have been five hundred of us sitting there, hopeless and voteless. Louis looked right in our faces and said, "Now, listen. There isn't anything we can do for you up here until you've done something for yourselves. If you don't have any voting power, there isn't *anything* we can do for you. These people are listening to where they get their votes from, not from where they get their aches, pains, hollering and suffering."

It was bitter medicine. I went back to Mississippi and started to work. We launched a voter registration drive and voted. If Louis had sugarcoated the problem, I probably wouldn't have done *anything*. He gave us the cold facts: "These people are politicians." I got so angry at Louis I could have shot him, but those were the facts. At that time we had less than 28,000 registered. Before 1965, to try to register in Mississippi was almost suicide. The white people were so bad they didn't allow us to register. They would kill and they would burn our homes. After the Voters Rights Bill, which Congress passed in 1965, they began to enforce the right to register and vote. Then black people began to register.

When President Johnson asked for the Voting Rights Bill, he told Congress, "The Negro citizen may go to register only to be told that the day is wrong, or the hour is late, or the official in charge is absent." Johnson is a favorite of mine. I'm against war 101 percent, and I've been against all wars, but we've been having wars—and wars, and wars, and wars. I'm not going to let Johnson's domestic programs be overshadowed by his stand on Vietnam. I admired him because he was a Southerner, and somehow he knew how to handle these Southern rascals. I'm proud that he cared enough and was big enough to carry out John Kennedy's program. I don't think you can say that about very many other presidents. President Johnson carried it out almost to the letter. Black folks should be the last to knock Johnson. That goes for Stokely Carmichael and H. Rap Brown.

It was Lyndon Johnson who put the Civil Rights bill through, who made it possible for us to eat in the hotels and motels and to get a drink of water out of any fountain. It was Lyndon Johnson who cared enough to push an old folk's hospitalization program. And had it not been for the president blacks wouldn't be able to go to a Southern hospital and be treated in a nonsegregated room, in a nonsegregated ward, with all the attention and respect that any other patient gets.

President Johnson named a Negro to his cabinet, Robert Weaver as Secretary of HUD; he appointed, among others, Carl Rowan Director of the United States Information Agency and Ambassador to Finland; Mrs. Patricia Roberts Harris Ambassador to Luxembourg; Lyle Carter Assistant Secretary of HEW; and Thurgood Marshall to the Supreme Court.

President Johnson walked on the floor of his inaugural ball and took a black woman—the wife of his special counsel—and asked her to dance with him. That's saying something. I don't care what anybody says, you couldn't have gotten another president to dance with a black woman.

Those Texas big-hat men that he knew, those Mississippians, Eastland and Stennis; Strom Thurmond, Talmadge, Russell and Long—they had been with him for years. He challenged them. When a man does that, you have to give him credit. It was because he was dedicated— and he knew all of them. They had been doing things together, and he probably had enough on them to say, "Now, wait there, buddy, I want this Civil Rights Bill passed."

Nelson Rockefeller of New York has done more for us than any governor in the United States. Give the man his due. His family's bank, the Chase Manhattan, has hired more black folks than any other bank in the country. Rocky has more black advisors than any other politician in the country. He stood by Jackie Robinson when some blacks and Jewish people got on Jackie's back for hiring some white people.

Now Arthur Goldberg was a nice man. But his running mate, Basil Patterson, was just another symbol. We need more symbols and tokens like we need more holes in our head. We need power and authority.

Probably the least appreciated of all the whites who have done good things for us is Senator Hubert H. Humphrey. Somehow we've never helped him get that big break he's deserved. When he was Vice President he had quite a few blacks working for him. He was fighting racism before it became fashionable. He's always spoken up on what he thought was right and wrong.

What bothers me about my people is that they've forgotten the bridge that carried us across, forgotten the guys who scratched our backs when we needed it scratched. They jump on the first loudmouth who comes along. Black folks are so easily misled by white folks. White folks start hollering and some of us join hands even though we don't know what we're joining. We just join.

I know Lyndon and Bobby hated each other, but that's a different thing. That had nothing to do with what they were doing. We have to be able to distinguish. Forget how they felt about each other. They were the loudest mouths in this country for poor folks. I don't care what anybody says. They showed concern for blacks, Mexicans and the poor. I couldn't care less about their personal relationship.

18

1965

Until 1965, everything in Mississippi was segregated and
blacks couldn't go into any of the public places. We made
up our minds after the Civil Rights Bill was passed that we
were going to desegregate all public accommodations. We
started in McComb and Walthall County. Cops and deputized white citizens of the community were there with
their guns. We went right on, we drove right through
them that day. They called us "niggers" and "black bas-
tards" and "you dirty-sons-of-bitches," but we went into
a McComb motel and ate, and we registered to spend the
night. This was the first time we had done that. They
must have had two or three hundred highway patrol watching. They saw we would die—or they would—before we
gave in to them.

In May 1965 we went into Natchez and desegregated all
the hotels there. There were about twenty of us in Natchez,

and three hundred rednecks. We were sitting in the Eola Hotel, trying to eat. We weren't hungry, but we were sitting in there and they were outside with knives and guns, just pecking on the windows, saying "We're going to get you. We're going to get you when you come out."

Chuck Quinn of NBC-TV and Reggie Smith of UPI and other reporters were there. They were scared, too. When we came out of the hotel, all of the klansmen met us at the door, but they began to back up as we walked out—and one thing about a racist is that if you look him in the eye and keep walking, he loses his courage. I was scared to death, but they didn't know it. Thomas Washington and Percy Chapman were behind me. Doris Allison—she's the former president of the Jackson branch of the NAACP—she was with me, and Mrs. Bell, one of our staunchest supporters.

One of the burly white racists had a shotgun and another one was coming toward me with a knife about a foot long, saying, "I'm gonna kill this sonofabitch." I was going to grab him if he tried to knife me. I was going to fly into him. But when he was within reach of me, Reggie Smith stepped between us and then Chuck Quinn stepped in with his camera. These newsmen were fearless. It was a story to them. They weren't stepping between us to protect me, but they had guts. This saved me from getting cut, because if the Kluxers had cut me every Negro would have turned that town inside out and a lot of people would have gotten killed right there. The bigots turned on the newsmen and chased them, and I got into my car and went on down to the Albert Pick Hotel, which we opened up that same night. I had all of my boys stationed at the Holiday Inn with rifles.

George Metcalf was the president of our branch in Natchez. George is the man who went with me during all of our desegregation activity. He's the one who carried the petition to desegregate the schools down to the Natchez Board of Education. George worked at the Armstrong Tire and Rubber plant. One night in the summer of 1965 he came out of the plant and got into his car to go home. And when he turned the switch on, the car blew up, but it didn't kill him.

During our protest in Natchez we had all sorts of problems. We went to the city and tried to get a permit to march, but they wouldn't give us a permit. We marched anyway. The Mayor said, "Just give me a little time, we'll give you a permit to march. We'll protect you if you march." The Klan in their sheets was riding around on horses and pointing their guns at every black. They were shooting into Negroes' homes. I told my people, "Listen, we're not going to run any more, and we're not going to take any more shootings. If they shoot us, we're going to shoot back."

We used a man named Russell in Natchez as sort of a guinea pig. He didn't know about TV cameras at that time, and he didn't know that he would be on national broadcasts. We put him on Mrs. Mazique's porch. He was raving, bragging about how he would shoot a white man, and Chuck Quinn and others were taping this. This is the sort of thing that frightens white people. They expected me to say it, but a local jackleg preacher would really have some effect on them. He went on and on, and Bob Evans of CBS and others had their reels flown to New Orleans. And that evening, on the regular news, Huntley-Brinkley ran it. When Russell saw it he almost had a hemorrhage. He knew that the white folks were going to come after him. We had guards around his house, and guards where I was living, at Mamie Lee Mazique's. The whites put curfews on us, but we broke them. We had guns and hand grenades, and everything it took to work with—and we meant to use them if we had to.

Then one night in Natchez, at a mass meeting an FBI man came to me and said, "Mr. Evers, I'd advise you not to go out that door tonight, because they're going to kill you."

I said, "Who are you to tell me they're going to come here to kill me! Can't you stop them?"

"No, our job is not to make arrests before but afterward."

"Well, I don't need you around here. Get the hell out of my face. I don't need anybody telling me somebody's going to kill me. Well, if they're going to kill me they got a chance," and I just walked on out the door. The guards and troopers were out there, and nothing happened.

Mrs. Mazique is a dear friend of mine. Her house in Natchez was the house we used. When no one else would take us in, she would. She'd just lost her husband, a good man. Everybody loved her and we sort of protected her. Mamie Lee Mazique has been unbelievable. In the first place, her husband left her in good shape financially. Her family believes in civil rights. She hid me any number of times. Back in those days the Klan was really trying to kill me. I'd always go in one place and out the back door, get in a car and go on down to her place and stay at her house. They would sit on the front porch and watch while I'd sleep—she and a group of the fellows we had. The white people didn't know how to attack Mrs. Mazique. She didn't have any mortgages or anything like that. And she owned about four or five rent houses.

Every time we'd go to a town like Natchez we'd give the city, the Chamber of Commerce, the Board of Education and the city school system certain demands we wanted them to meet, and we'd give them a certain date to meet them. We'd say: *Integrate all the school facilities, hire blacks as clerks in the stores, hire black policemen, black deputy sheriffs.* We would take them town by town.

One of our twelve demands was that Negroes be addressed as "Mr." or "Mrs." or "Miss," and that they quit calling us "niggers" and "boy" and "girl" and "auntie" and "hoss." But this was something the bigots never could agree to. We gave them ten days to meet our demands, and then we started our marching and picketing and slapped our boycotts on the town. What we're saying by boycotting is: *White folks, get your foot off our neck. White folks, turn loose some of that money and let us have some jobs. White folks, give us some better schools. White folks, let us have a part in the policy-making. White folks, we're just as good as you are.*

George Metcalf was still in the hospital, and the entire Negro community united. All elements were together with one single purpose, and the boycott was almost 100 percent effective.

There in Natchez we made our greatest score in the economic and political field when we desegregated twenty-plus stores at one time. They hired black clerks, they hired black policemen—the ones we chose—with the rights to police all sections of the town, both white and black. We made them hire black salesmen on the beer trucks and pop trucks and on the bread trucks. We never had this before. This is what the dollar can do, this is what the boycott can do. If black people in this country would just realize the importance of sticking together! This is how we get what we get in Mississippi. We had our protective squad. We had all our own guns. We didn't go around bragging about it, but we were ready to enforce those boycotts, to die if necessary. And they knew we were ready. And we'd do it all over.

That's how we got black policemen in Jackson. Negroes hired to help school-children at street crossings. We got black people working in the stores. We saw to it that blacks can stay in any hotel or motel. All of these were our grievances. No more cursing and calling anybody nigger by the police. They'd better not call us that.

In 1965, Aaron Henry and I were jailed in Clarksdale. I haven't said much about Aaron, but he has stood the test. He's been my adviser, brother, friend. He's been my lawyer, he's been everything that I need, and without him Mississippi would not have moved the way it has. Now, I can't take a lot of abuse, but Aaron can. The racists put Aaron in jail. They put about twenty of us in one cell. I told them, "Hell, I'm going to get out of here. I'm not going to stay in here." So I bailed myself out.

But Aaron stayed there for a whole week, in July, and it was in the nineties and hundreds every day, and all Aaron was guilty of was that he'd marched and wanted the right to be a part of the community. Aaron never stopped smiling. When they bombed his house—Congressman Diggs was there at the time—Aaron kept saying, "Don't hate them. We're going to get them. Don't hate them." The charge was a question of the right of free speech. It had to do with parading without a permit to address our grievances to the Mayor and the city councilmen. There must have been about 250 of us who went to jail. Reverend J. Rayford was there, and Cleo Jackson, Robert Pettus. Lillian Rodgers Johnson, Jim Gilliam, David Self, Jr., Vera Pigee. I was concerned mostly about Aaron, because I didn't figure anybody else was in as much physical danger as he was. And after I was out on bail I went and saw the work they had him doing—cleaning out the commodes, and then they chained him to a garbage truck and made him hobble through the streets picking up garbage. I called the NAACP in New York and told them Aaron should get out, so they sent me to talk him into coming out. Just before I got to Aaron, I heard one of the rednecks cursing him out: "If niggers like you was run out of town, we'd have a better town!"

I said, "Aaron, for God's sake, I've got the bail money. Let's get the hell out of here."

"No, Charley," he said, and he just kept smiling.

I was never so angry at anybody in all my life. He just wouldn't leave.

Only God kept us. You better believe it, brother. The kind of things that black people here have lived through, only God could have saved us.

There's so much work to be done in Mississippi that I have to spend all of my time right here.

19

Our devils haven't changed any. We're still chasing the same ones—the political devil, the economic devil, the racist devil. The most important thing is to know where you're going. Those Northern folks don't know where the hell they're going. They're so suppressed and depressed that everything is wrong. They haven't helped the movement at all, because they resist doing what must be done—getting organized and *voting*. In our political rallies we discuss issues. We want to get the voting age in Mississippi lowered to eighteen. The first issue we've dealt with is the war. We're beginning to get blacks on Mississippi draft boards for the first time. We can't change things by getting angry. We can't change things by giving up. We cause change by pushing, as we have in the past.

I think to fight a war in Vietnam and to shoot Negroes down in Mississippi is all the same thing. I don't

want to participate in any war. I went because I had to go.
I wouldn't go again in this kind of war, because it's wrong.
Somewhere, as individuals, we've got to take a stand.
That's why I admire Muhammed Ali for what he did. He
lost a whole lot of material things, but his soul is satisfied
and his heart is right. That's what really counts with a
man. You've got to *believe* and to be willing to pay the
price. Vietnam's been a useless and senseless war. We have
no business being there.

I asked Negroes to refuse induction into the armed
forces until state draft boards are desegregated. There's not
a white person in Mississippi who would allow his son to
be drafted by an all-Negro draft board. It's not fair for us
to be called by all-white ones.

The system in Mississippi is beginning to crack a little.
It's not opening, but it's cracking. It's going to get a little
wider and wider. All we've got to do is keep pushing and
not lose our heads and become hate-mongers. We're going
to make it open. We're going to pry it open with our votes,
our dollars, our education and our determination to make
Mississippi a better place for all of us.

There's a need for extending the Voting Rights Act beyond 1975 because once we lose it then the state's going to
go back and enact its own laws as the Kluxers did before,
and they'll disenfranchise all black people. So we must
have the continuation of the Voting Rights Act. If you de-
feat that, then you're really going to have trouble in this
country because we will not have any hope. Our hope is
through voting, through education and through the economic process. If you take that away from us, we're
through. Charles Evers, Aaron Henry, Julian Bond and
others will not be able to save this country. One thing
about this act bothers me: I think a person who can't read
or write should be able to carry into the poll with him
a person of his choice. If I've got to go into the booth with

someone the election commission has chosen, then I don't feel free. Maybe I want to vote for a candidate that my boss doesn't want me to vote for. Maybe I've got every reason in the world to know that the white racist there to "help" me is going to tell my boss who I voted for. It's not right. And besides, how do I know that this man "helping" me is pulling the lever for the candidate I want? That's really how we lost the municipal election in Woodville in 1969.

Today we're on the juries in Mississippi. And we've learned that if you can't win, hang it. It takes only one man to hang the jury. If we just get one on there, that's enough. One man will say, "I'm not going to change my mind." The white folks taught us that. If you can hang a jury and free one of yours, we can hang a jury and free one of ours. That's going to make somebody start doing justice. This is the kind of thing we're teaching our people.

I think most of us are very much in doubt about the corrections of any of our ills. I believe in law and order. The difference is that I believe in law and order and justice for everybody. In the past one could bootleg if he wanted to, long as he was white or backed by the sheriff or backed by the Mayor or by some of the top officials. Now we're going to make sure we have law and order. We're going to make sure that the housing administration will not deny a black man the right to have a house because he's black. This is part of law and order. We're going to make sure all our schools are completely integrated and open to anybody. We're going to enforce the law as it's written.

I am an integrationist. And I hope that this administration from the President on down will understand that they've got to set an example of leadership to include all of the people who want to be a part of the system.

20

On January 10, 1962, Vernon Dahmer, an NAACP leader, was burned to death in the fire-bombing of his home in Hattiesburg, Mississippi. I remember the times when Vernon and I went up and down the road in Hattiesburg. We worked very close there, and he had just been made, the week before, chairman of our voter-registration drive. When I heard Vernon had been killed it took something out of me, because I was one of those who had asked Vernon to take the job.

Hattiesburg was such a hard place to bring around to the Civil Rights Act of 1964 and the Voting Rights Act of 1965. The bigots assassinated Vernon over the question of our collecting poll taxes for people who were afraid to go down and pay their own tax. Later, under the leadership of Dr. C. E. Smith, Hattiesburg got in line with other integrated communities. The racists killed Vernon Dahmer and Clyde Kennard. Those were two we knew about. How many others were killed and dumped in the forest, rivers and creeks around the area? Not only in Hattiesburg, but in other parts of the South. You don't know how many blacks have been killed. The white murderers are free and bragging about their killings. It's because there have been so many deliberate murders of Negroes like Vernon Dahmer that some blacks want to hate and to burn and to kill. It was in Mississippi that Stokely first used the slogan "Black Power." The crackers locked us up—this was during the first Meredith march in 1966—and then they released us. As soon as Stokely was released he started hollering, "Burn the damned jail."

I said, "Stokely, we were just released from jail. Now, why didn't you burn it while you were in there?"

My people are trying to tell you white people a truth, but you won't listen. Black folks are fighting a war, and our wants are the same: *White folks, get your feet off our necks.* We have one goal, but we use different methods for getting there. I'm not fighting my black brothers, but the white devil, the evil system that's keeping us down. Let's not think there was no one before us. Who am I to say, "I'm the man who saved Mississippi?" I'd be crazy. We're all struggling, sneaking around and trying to do the things to make it better for Negroes ever since there's been a Mississippi. I'd be a damn fool to think that Medgar and Charles Evers were the only ones who ever made a contribution to Mississippi.

The preacher, the teacher and the deacon in the church have been doing their thing to make it better for my children. They prayed for us, they tricked white folks for us, they grinned at them and cursed them out at the same time for us, in order to get enough food to feed us. But the young folks, they don't see this. They want somebody with a prescribed solution. Well, hell, five years ago these same youngsters, if they'd opened their mouths, they would have been buried like Schwerner, Chaney and Goodman were.

People like my brothers in the NAACP, those of us who kept hammering away, are the ones who made it possible for these kids to holler now. For a black person and a white person to sit in a restaurant even five years ago and have breakfast together, or even talk together, was suicide. If a white woman sat in a café with Negroes, the Kluxers would have been riding up and down the road. They would have dragged her out for some lynching parties.

The young people don't realize that they're not the beginning of the civil rights movement. It goes way back—like the oldest resident in the county, J. P. Lewis. He sold me the land for my shopping center in Fayette when nobody would sell me land. "I'll sell it to you, son," he said. "I want you to stay here with us and help us, because I've been here a long time." They threatened him, an old man like that! And the black kids say, "He's a Tom." He's not a Tom. The young black militants come along with: "You're out of tune." These loudmouths don't do anything but confuse somebody and get somebody killed. My argument with the loudmouths is that one day white folks are going to make you stand up to them. White folks bluffed us a long time. They fooled the hell out of us and scared us until we called their bluff. The whites didn't do anything. Oh, they killed two or three of us, but we came back. They bombed us, but we kept coming.

I think that 98 percent of the black people in this country believe the way I believe. I tell the black militants not to ridicule my people. Just take on and take off. I'm trying to pick up where Medgar dropped and keep going. I'm certainly going to give Medgar and all those people credit for what they did. They got us this far. So I tell the young folks, "Don't come here shouting, 'Everybody's a Tom this' and 'Everybody's a Tom that.' If it hadn't been for us you wouldn't be here. We're the ones who kept the civil rights movement going, otherwise you wouldn't even know what civil rights is."

At a speaking engagement some young blacks came up to me and wanted to know why I was so concerned about helping Whitey. And I said, "Let me tell you one thing. If you think the way I believe is wrong, then you prove to me your way is better." There was about a dozen of them, with beards. I said, "Yes, I'm going to defend white folks, and black folks, if they're right. And I'll knock hell out of any black or white who I know is wrong."

They asked, "Why don't you look out for black folks? All you talk about is working together."

I replied, "Wait a minute. Who does this building belong to?"

"It probably belongs to some honky."

"No, it belongs to some white American who thinks enough to let you stay in here."

"We're paying rent."

"Where you get the money from?"

"Well, we got a grant from . . ."

"Yeah, now name me one black foundation. Name me *one* black foundation."

"Well, if they give us the money *it's because* they owe us."

"No one owes you one penny. No one owes you anything but a chance. This back-pay you're talking about is baloney. Don't anybody owe us nothing but a chance. Nobody is going to back-pay the Jews, nobody is going to back-pay the Italians, nobody is going to back-pay the Indians, and ain't nobody going to back-pay the Negro in this country. All we want is a chance, you better remember that. Because all that big bad talk ain't going to get you nothing but a bullet right through your head from some of those racists out here or some of those policemen."

They kept talking about the honkies, so I said, "Man what are you talking about these whiteys? Haven't any of you suffered the way I've suffered from white folks. But that doesn't give you any right to hate them. My job is to stop hate. And you don't stop whitey by getting like him. You stop him by doing something different than what he has done."

"Well, we're going to go to Mississippi."

"I'm going to have law and order in Fayette. You come down there and if you break the law, you are going to jail and there isn't going to be any bail, because I'm the judge and the jury. Don't you forget that."

I went out, got in the car and left. They stood there at the window. You just can't hate. It's not enough. You got to have a conviction. And you got to stand by it. When whitey rubs you wrong, get him off you. When blackey rubs you wrong, get him off you. But you can't run over anybody, and you can't let anybody run over you. That's my feeling. I ain't going to let anybody run over me. No-o-o.

I won't take polarization from anybody, including blacks. The extremist groups will never have political success. And political success is what counts. The Panthers will have no more success than the Klan did. Fear and hate will not survive, whether it's blacks or whites who're doing the fearing and hating.

I'm not about to go from white slavery into black slavery. The Panthers would deny me the right to do what I want to do. That's just what white racists say, "Do it my way or no way." I don't want to go round calling people honky, pig or shoot people. Don't tell *me* to do that. I've fought my whole life against discrimination.

I may be a capitalist, but those rascals are, too, and don't let them tell you different. Sleeping with all those blue-eyed millionaire blonde girls. Riding around with movie stars in their Cadillacs. It amazes me how the white folks fall for their line. Especially when they insult them so much.

All this talk about guns. They don't have enough guns to kill ten rabbits anywhere. They only got enough vocal guns to frighten folks. Show me three places where they've gone in and destroyed what they call the pigs and the honkies. Three places. They bash you all over the place with their words. But their shotguns wouldn't kill an old sick dog running down the road.

We used to call it bluff, but today they call it psychological warfare. All that long hair does is scare some people.

There are a few confused blacks and whites who'll say a kind word for them, but all they're doing is widening the gap between white folks, black folks, Mexican folks and Jewish folks. And that just means more trouble.

During the march for James Meredith, Stokely Carmichael came with us for a head-on confrontation with the National Guard and the Highway Patrol about 20 miles north of Jackson in Canton.

I warned our people: These guys don't play around. If you don't mean it and aren't ready to back up what you say, don't provoke them.

So there was old Stokely, raving and cussing and raising sand. All of a sudden they kaloo that teargas into us. Stokely started screaming like a drowning rat:

"Ahhhhhh! Ooooooo! Eeeeeee! ! They're going to kill us all!"

I said, "Go on, Stokely. Go back. Go back to the house. Go on, now, baby, cool down. Take it easy."

I gave it to him later on. "You talk so damned tough. Don't hand me that tough crap. And don't talk that crap to my folks. Because you don't mean it. Tell the white man what you want him to know. But be fair and firm.

[145]

You don't have to prove anything except that you mean what you say by your actions."

And old Floyd McKissick, talking about building this "Soul City" of his. Begging all the white folk for their money. Yet he says he doesn't want any "honkies" around. That's crap, too. The white man'll own 51 per cent of it and he'll get one-fifth. He's fooling the white folks but he's not fooling me.

Eldridge Cleaver is a genuine talent, but a wasted talent. What good is his knowledge doing us over in Algiers or some damn place? Same as Rap Brown with all that loud big mouth talk. How much better a job he'd have done if he'd work to change things rather than inflame them. If he'd been firm and precise. If he'd gone to Alabama or Georgia, county by county. And gotten black folks to realize how important it is to take over the sheriffs, the mayors, the constables, and the like.

One good thing the extremists are doing is to give the people a clear choice between them and us. They're forcing people to make up their minds, shocking them with their violence into realizing that we can't have either black or white extremism.

We're all saying the same thing, though. We're saying that our mommas, our daddies, our grandfolks all begged you, prayed to you, but you never heard a word they were saying. You killed them. You lynched them. You buried them. And you all read about it in the newspapers. If it's really an eye-for-an-eye that you want, we'll give that to you.

I have some respect for the Muslims, though, even though they're not Christians. But they're all clean livers. They're doers. They're quiet. They just move in and take over, baby. They've got schools, all kinds of industry, bakeries, clothing stores, supermarkets, cattle ranches. And it's *theirs*.

There's a world of difference between them and the Panthers, who talk big and bad and tough. What's happened to the Panthers so far? They have had their own butts whipped and run over, their own shacks burned and shot up. That's what.

We never would have gotten as far as we have in Mississippi if we had the attitude of the white extremists or the attitude of the black extremists. One group says that all white folks are wrong and the other group says that all black folks are wrong. As I say to my white friends, "Don't try to brand us. We have as much right to have nuts in our race as you do in yours." It's up to us, the whites and the blacks, the rich and the poor, to join hands to overshadow the extremists of both races. We've got to know where we're going and let nothing stand in the way. Killing Medgar did more to move us ahead than anything else. We lost one of us—and Medgar understood this a long time ago. We've said a lot of times and we still say, "It's not important how long a man lives, it's what he does while he's here."

A lot of my brothers are saying integration won't work, and I think their disenchantment was brought about because it hasn't worked. That's because our white brothers haven't let it work. But we've got to have it work. This is no country for separatism. We can't live separate. Because there is no way in the world that we can live in America without coming in contact with white people. White people can't live here without coming in contact with black people. My belief is that if we just keep doing worthwhile things we can make integration work.

It's easy to say, "Aw, it isn't going to work. It hasn't worked," and then give up. It's hard to keep hammering away, to keep fighting to get the things we believe in. But we're doing it, and it's going to work. White folks, don't let the blacks fool you. Muhammed Ali doesn't want anything separate. He has proven that. A large number of white folks are saying Muhammed Ali wants all blacks to be separate. But listen: Ali made his money by fighting white folks. And you know where Ali lives? You go and see where Ali lives. And most of the blacks who've hollered for separatism have white girl friends. At the time Stokely was hollering about black separatism, someone went and got him—you know where they found him? In his white girlfriend's apartment. Rap Brown was fooling around with a white woman.

This reminds me of what the racists down South have been doing for so long: Hollering "nigger!" during the day and sleeping black all night. There's a lot of that kind of hypocrisy among the white and black extremists. And we're not going to have it.

When the black militants went into Lowndes County they talked big. But you can't get elected by talking big. You get elected by votes. They didn't get votes in Lowndes County. It's the same way all over the country. In Jefferson County we organized and we talked big, but we backed it up. And we won. Carrying guns and threatening people don't win elections. All you do is drive voters away.

You see, my folks are sick and tired of racism. They're tired of hearing hate, tired of hearing "We're going to take it all." They want a man who says, "Let's bring our community together." We're not about to go and vote for any black folks or any white folks who preach hatred and destruction.

My folks want to hear in Mississippi, "Let's work together." We're going to keep preaching that. We're going to get you whites together whether you like it or not.

Someone asked me, "How long can you keep talking nonviolence?"

It's very simple: If my way is not the way, what's the

answer? *Burning it down?* If we're not going to learn to live and work together, what are we going to do? If it won't work, what will work? Are we going to destroy our towns and our communities?

Now, young blacks, let's not fool ourselves. This country wasn't made for separatism. Any white man who tells you to get in a corner—he ain't your friend. And that's what he has pretty well done so far.

Someone asked me, "Would you as a black American want to go back to Africa?" Well, now, I don't know anything about Africa. I was born and reared in America, and I'm not going "back" to Africa. I think those who are going to Africa should find out first of all if the Africans want them. A lot of black people say they're going but a lot of Africans are just as bitter against American Negroes as they are against the American whites. After all, Africa belongs to the African people, not the American. And I want to be remembered as nothing else but an American. I don't go along with the idea black folks have got to have African looks. Have your *own* look. Do what *you* want to do. No, I'm not going to Africa. No, I don't see any good I can do in Africa. I'm trying to make America right. I know what we have in America. I don't know a thing about Africa.

Now, some white folks like to justify their racism. They like to say, "A few hardships do you good. Give you personality and character." Sure. But being a Negro in a white world is something no white man can understand. It's horrible. And look at the black men and women the whites have crushed. I'm a great friend of Leontyne Price, who was born over at Laurel. But there's a hundred like her who were killed, one way or another, by this white man's field-slave, house-slave system. Just imagine all the blacks who've had great potential and were never able to develop because of the harassment they were subjected to. These evils of the white system have forced the black man to spend all his energies on just physically surviving. But if he had been made a part of the system, and was wanted and respected, he could have spent his life constructively.

And look at Eldridge Cleaver, who spends his time running and dodging the law because white America never gave him any reason to want to be a part of this country. And look at Stokely, who could be anybody's president of anything. He also decided that "it ain't worth it" because white America never gave him a chance to be a part of it. Most of my people are beginning to say, "What the hell?" And they'd rather go the other way—toward bitterness and hatred and destruction. That's why I hope I can hang on. But I don't know how long I can take it.

The young blacks and the young whites aren't going to take the hypocrisy. The young blacks in the army with all those howitzers and grenades could start an insurrection that would turn that army inside out. You can't tell the President anything and you can't tell the Congress anything and you can't tell the white racists anything. But if they keep on, they could destroy this country.

I was in Jackson the other day, coming from a meeting right across from the state office building. And I saw about thirty kids drilling, and two of them were black. They were drilling their hearts out. And I looked up at the office windows and saw all these whites staring, the people were driving along, staring. And I thought if we'd just leave them alone they would never think about color. Then I caught myself: I was staring, too. It's one of those things where all of us are guilty of wondering if it will work. When we see it working we all question it, including me. But it was fascinating to see those two black boys drilling with all those white boys, working together as Americans.

My idea for school integration was to integrate first-graders first. When the 1954 Supreme Court decision was passed, I was one of the first who said it wouldn't work. And I was called an Uncle Tom, a white folks' nigger. I said, "Listen, you call me what you want to call me, but it's not going to work. If you're saying that you're going to integrate every grade in the school, you're going to find that none of them are going to be integrated as they should." My feeling is that you just don't jump from the bottom to the top. I know it sounds like saying that "it takes time." It *does* take time. But we don't want to hide behind the fact that it takes time and not do anything. We have to accomplish the right kind of integration. I said that I'd like to see the Supreme Court enforce integration in every first grade in 1955, and then the second grade the next year, the third grade, and the fourth grade until every grade in this country is integrated. But when you take eleventh-graders and put them together, they've already got built-in prejudices and you're going to cause conflict. But had they used my plan, look where we'd be today. Every classroom in this country would be integrated and we would be on our way toward understanding each other. Those who were six years old would now be grown.

When I came out of school as a black schoolteacher in Noxapater, Mississippi, I made $19 a month, and that was considered good pay for a Negro. Now black teachers make about $3,500 a year in Mississippi with some making about $6,000. We need good teachers who think black. Those who will talk to our youngsters and advise them and tell them about the black man's blood that flowed during the Revolution, and about the Negro who invented the cotton gin, and the black men who navigated Columbus and got him over here. Let's demand black studies, but let the whites be the ones who get most of it. They're the ones who need to know.

We should have many more black instructors. I was at an Eastern college and there were 150-plus faculty members, and just one black among them. This doesn't make any kind of sense. We've got to open these doors. The college is a Christian college, and there's only one black working there. *One.* This is wrong. And they had one black study, which was elective.

But do you know what's wrong? The white historians. Had they written about how *all* of us built America, how the black people helped to lay the rails and clear the forest to California, how we helped to develop education, how we were the first to percolate coffee, then maybe we wouldn't have to tell it to you now. They've projected us as somebody who's looting, somebody who's stealing, somebody who's dirty. I think black-studies programs should be compulsory, that the program should be taught from the college freshman year through the senior year. And I'm against separatism any way it comes—that even goes for black studies.

Someone said, "Well, those Negro teachers in Mississippi ain't no good. They don't participate, they don't do anything in the freedom movement." But he was wrong. There's not a black schoolteacher or a parent that doesn't want the same thing that all the rest of us wanted. Black want the same thing that all the rest of us want. Black teachers have a job to do. Help other black folks fill out income-tax reports so they don't have to pay a white man $5. You ought to fill it out for poor black folks free. Hold sessions during January and February: "Free income-tax service." And, black teachers, let me say this: Had it not been for those poor, ignorant black folks who marched in the streets and challenged the white man, you schoolteachers wouldn't have any jobs. You've got to realize the debt you owe to those who risked their lives.

I also believe that Negroes should have a preparatory

tutoring service for those of us like myself who didn't get the type of education we needed. There should be classes that would prepare us to go to the best universities. Blacks like me who went to one-room Mississippi shacks, we're not prepared, we didn't have the education. You see, I know what it is to have no education, or little education—that's me. I went to college, but I couldn't pass a stiff grammar school test to this day. I don't make any bones about it. While attending college, I was not exposed to chemistry, business administration and other foundation courses. I received a degree from Alcorn A&M that's the equivalent of a good eighth grade education—*maybe*. So I know what inferior education can mean, and that's why I don't teach school. But for those who do teach, there are some who don't know that there were Negro teachers who risked their lives and their jobs and everything else so that they could challenge the system. It was a black teacher, Gladys Noel Bates, who filed the first suit for equal pay for black teachers. And they ran her out of Mississippi.

21

After I opened the Medgar Evers Shopping Center in 1966, the black shoppers came by the dozens to buy their groceries, and the whites in Jefferson County were so angry they could have died. They don't want to think that a Negro is doing something. They want us to stay on handouts. And then they say, "Niggers standin' around beggin', doing nothin'."

We've got to teach our people to buy from the black man, to carry their clothes to the black cleaners, buy their groceries from a black man, to let a black man bury them—and when a black man runs for office, to vote for the black man. This is what white America has done. They've done a helluva job convincing black folks that the black man isn't qualified to become mayor of a town. Or running a bank. The black man isn't capable of running a department store or a grocery store or holding any position of leadership. And I think what I'm doing now, teaching Negroes to become self-reliant and self-dependent, does more than any killing I might have done to avenge Medgar.

At the Medgar Evers Shopping Center we have twenty people working. I can't pay them much, but at least I pay them $1.25 an hour. When I opened the shopping center, blacks were making $6 and $7 per week—*per week*. The man I hired as a butcher was making $25 a week, seven days a week. He started with me at $75 a week. That doesn't sound like much, but you have to remember that blacks in Fayette have been earning an average of only $485 a year.

Today there's no point in my hollering that I can't get a cup of coffee at the Holiday Inn or sleep at the Heidelburg Hotel. That's not true anymore. We're at another step, and that's to become involved and be a part of the overall operation of our country. All we're doing now is going up the ladder. We're not going to keep marching up and down the street saying we can't do this, we can't do that, because that's over. We've accomplished that. There are still roadblocks in our path, though. You can open up all the hotels and all the motels you want to, but if you don't have the $8 or $10 or $15 to pay, you can't get in there. So there's the all-important matter of money.

We know how the white devils worked us. On the railroads they would work us for twelve hours a day and pay us a lousy 25¢ an hour. We remember when we got a *dime an hour*. And we'd better not get sassy or we wouldn't get that. We've had no chance at all at slicing up that pie. And now we're telling him: That pie is not all for you. We're going to help you slice it. We want our share. But we're not going to get it until we keep our money in our pocket and go spend it in black stores. So, black brothers, wake up. We've got freedom down the road. We've got to get up and go after it. Get registered, vote, vote together, vote for the man who's going to help all of us. If we start doing that, we'll get somewhere. Somebody open a grocery store; blacks support our folks. Stay out of the white man's store. Go spend your money with your own folks.

Industry could do more in one month than civil rights organizations could do in ten years just by saying, "Look, this is our policy: We are going to hire according to ability and not according to race. We'll give every man an equal chance to do whatever job he's qualified to do, or the job he can be trained to do." It's up to the executives of corporations to make rules and then whoever breaks them can be removed and someone replace him that will carry them out. When industry has come to the South it has followed the rules laid out by the old segregationists. He has to have only one washroom for black ladies and white ladies, and one washroom for black men and white men. There should be one salary scale—that is, according to what your job is. Let there be a foreman of any race, a man who can handle and control men, a man who can produce. Again I say, it's up to management and the labor unions. It's in the white man's hands, and if he doesn't do it we're really doomed. Let's face it. What can we really do? Sure, we could go out and kill some white folks. But they can annihilate all of us. If we become violent, we're through.

You see, I believe that somewhere the white man still has a conscience and wants to be converted, wants to believe that love is stronger than hate.

A klansman died of aplastic anemia in Fayette recently. All his blood left him while he was still alive and he turned plumb white. He was forty-eight years old, but he had beaten Negroes and helped to kill Negroes. He shot at an old Negro woman going up the road and he came to Ferd Allen's place of business—Allen is our branch NAACP president—and asked him to get in his car—he was going to take him out and kill him, too. Ferd wouldn't go. He told the racist, "I know you're out to kill me, but you're through killing Negroes." Later on the klansman became sick. God, he suffered. When the doctors told him he was out of blood, he begged, "Get me any blood. I don't care what kind of blood it is. Just get me some blood. I want to live." He would have been glad to get blood from a red man, a white man, a black man—any kind of blood.

22

On February 27, 1967, in Natchez, Worlest Jackson, one of our NAACP leaders, was killed by a bomb planted in his car. Worlest was a close friend of George Metcalf, and I've already told about how the hate-mongers planted a bomb in George's car. Somehow he came out of it alive. But Worlest was killed. When I saw him dead, I remembered when we had started the branch together in Natchez. He was treasurer. The Sunday before he was killed he came to Fayette and asked me how we would change white men's hearts. We believe the killers were the same racists who tried to kill George Metcalf. And to this day none of them has paid for the crime. That's what has given whites the feeling that they have the right to go out and kill black folks.

Organization is important. The one thing I can do is go in and organize communities. When I organize communities I automatically organize Evers as a part of the community. I'm good about that and I know it, and I brag about it. But I don't take over the community. Ask Port Gibson. Ask Natchez, because we worked together. We don't make a move without each other. It's a sort of tie-in. Woodville and Hazlehurst and Crystal Springs are the same way. I think it's a matter of where you place your emphasis, and if you really want to work. If you're out for glamour, well, you're going to have problems.

Someone asked me, "What would happen to the people here in Mississippi if you got killed?" I think if it happened right now it would be a tragedy, because the people haven't yet been able to get a grasp of things, where they can go for themselves. The average education has been less than fifth grade. The people are just now beginning to get the feeling they can do things for themselves. They've had a lot of distrust in themselves, because of what the whites taught them. They bewildered their minds and souls. For centuries my people were told, "You are inferior to the white. And you can't do anything about it. God planned it that way."

Our fight for freedom is the proudest chapter in America's history. Take the folks in Jefferson County. Some of the "well-off" Negroes make between $1,000 and $1,500 a year. A bricklayer who built the Medgar Evers Shopping Center probably makes something like that. He doesn't make much, because he works only seasonally. You might ask, "How do people survive?" Well, it's a funny thing how some people can survive on little or nothing. With an income of only $1,000 a year, most of these people own cars. They don't wear Stacy Adams shoes, nor do they wear Kuppenheimer suits, but they all wear clothes, and they all eat, and they all drink. But where white people eat steaks we eat neck bones and maybe where white people eat cereal for breakfast we have a bowl of rice or some "fat" meat. It's hard to believe that in this day in America there are still people who don't get enough to eat. But that's a fact. And where white people go out for dinner and spend $5 or $6, maybe we go home and eat some black-eyed peas and some cornbread and some ham hocks. So we've been able to adjust ourselves to our incomes. Fresh bread costs you 36¢, but you can go to the bakery the next day and get that same loaf for 15¢. The blacks help each other, and in Mississippi we trust each other. I never lock my doors. I just don't think anybody would come in and bother me. When my stores are open, I seldom go in there. I don't worry about my people doing anything but good for me. And they know I'm trying to do good for them. The black people have had to understand each other, to love one another, in order to survive. Anytime I get sick, I don't worry. I just have to pick up the phone and four or five dozen friends are at the door. And I'm the same way with them. It's not because I'm Charles Evers, but just because that's the way we are. Any person who gets sick here, well, we all go and see about him.

If black people believe in you, if you prove you're truthful, there's nothing my people won't do for you. *Nothing*. That's why I've been able to do what I have. My people protect me. That's why I'll never be bought, by anybody. I don't have to be bought, because I can get anything I want from my people. All I have to do is want it and need it. If I need something today and don't have it—if I needed $50,000 this day—give me ten days and I'd get it. It's taken time to build this kind of faith. To begin with, the people believed in Medgar. But their trust in me didn't just happen. In the past, so many others have come along and lied and disappointed them. So it's natural you still find some people wondering if it's really true: Does Charles Evers care enough to go out and work for their welfare? It seems as if, each time the black people have gotten good leaders, they were apt to be bought off or frightened off. This killed the faith we had in them, so the white people took over and gave all the directions.

I'm not *the* leader, and I don't want to be *the* leader in Mississippi. We're trying to build leaders in each of the communities. Anything can happen to me tomorrow. I've always known that.

To me politics means doing what's possible. My theory is that life is so short and time is so precious that it doesn't make sense to waste any of it on something you know you can't do anything about. So I try to eliminate some of the things we don't like, and get rid of some of the things we're not satisfied with, and work to accomplish some of the benefits we want. I have very little respect for anyone, black or white, who talks big and bad and later on has nothing to show for it. I never forgot some of the things Daddy taught Medgar and me. He said, "Don't never criticize or tear up nothin' unless you got somethin' better to offer." That's what I live by.

Once you get into politics you go as far as you can. So I'm not going to say that I'm not going to run for president. Who wouldn't like to be President of the United States? Lester Maddox was a confused man, but a lucky man, the time he ran for governor. But he has had his day. We're going to get together and we're going to start a new country. Those loudmouthed blacks and loudmouthed whites, we're going to stop them. We're going to stop them not by trying to suppress them with guns, but by outdoing them, by doing the things a man was meant to do. We're on our way.

You know, George Wallace is a smart politician, but a lazy man. He doesn't want to work. And he knows the easiest way in the world to make an easy living is to go up in the wild hollows and make a couple of racist talks and maybe run for governor or run for president.

[161]

When you stand up as an old Southern racist, you collect the dollars. Wallace knows people are gullible, and his party will probably continue, but it's not going to be as forceful and as active as it has been. I expected him to get more votes, because you would be surprised at the number of people in the country that think the way Wallace does. The only reason he didn't get more was that he took on LeMay for his running mate. People were afraid that LeMay might drop a bomb on New York, and another on Chicago, and one on Jackson. Even those who would have voted for Wallace got scared of LeMay. That was *too much* "law and order." They could take Wallace but they sure couldn't take LeMay.

Really, there are few if any white politicians on the national scene that the black man in the South can respect. I sort of like Fulbright. He has not been very liberal on civil rights, but he has been a liberal about Vietnam. As far as I know, he was one of the first who spoke out against the war. I wouldn't vote for him if there was someone else, but he has done some good things. Traditionally, those Dixie politicians have played on the gullibility of the Southern whites. You have to remember that the racist politicians in Mississippi have held down all the people, not just the blacks; and they're too stiff-backed to take government money to help poor people.

There are so many ways blacks can lose an election in the South. In the first place, we shouldn't take it for granted that just because the blacks have a majority in some communities that a black candidate is automatically going to win. A good example was in our election in Fayette. We had everything it really took to win an election, yet we were frightened to death because we had to make sure *our* people were convinced that we could run a town. Another reason the black man can lose is fear of reprisals, particularly economic reprisals, where the white people say they're going to foreclose the mortgage on your home or on your business, or where they're going to get you fired from your job. Around Fayette, where most of my people are on welfare, the blacks were told, "If you vote for Evers and his slate you're going to lose your welfare check." That's why I knew there was a great chance of me losing—not because they didn't want to vote for me, but because they were afraid.

23

My race for Congress in 1968 was one of those unexpected ventures. I hadn't planned to be involved in politics that way. I had never been an elected official. But I was drafted by the third congressional district, which included twelve counties. You see, this is the second largest black district in the state. My people asked me if I would run. We needed a candidate, and I happened to be the one they chose. So I ran, and we had a good time with it. A lot of white people had never really heard a Negro list the things that blacks really wanted.

We won the first primary. We beat by 7,500 votes in the first primary, but we had run against five or six whites, and when we eliminated them that left the two top vote-getters for a runoff: Charley Griffin and me. The whites put their votes together and beat me by almost two to one. I received 43,000 votes and Charley Griffin got about

80,000. We felt the mere fact that we got Negroes out to vote was victory by itself.

In running for Congress I was able to bring out some issues that had never been raised before. As a result, I received a few white votes and 99 percent of the black vote. My running for Congress gave Negroes hope. Before, when there was a white issue or a white candidate the white people didn't like, they'd say, "By God, we're going fishing." So we said, "You go fishing if you want." And we meant it. They knew they had better not go fishing—or they would wake up and find a black man for their congressman.

This was a special election, because John Bell Williams left the Congress to become the state's new governor in January 1968. Usually in a special election like this not many of the people vote. But this time about 80 or 85 percent of the people voted. Everyone knew that Griffin's 80,000 votes in the runoff were votes for a white candidate against a black one. They didn't know whether I was going to make a good congressman or not, but many of them wanted to give me a chance. A lot of whites started thinking and listening to our side, and they realized they had been wrong. The Congressional race was a great step forward, and Mississippi will never be the same, because we're going to vote and we're going to elect people—good people, black and white—who are going to do what's right.

The third district includes Jackson. Television played a big role in this election, just as it does in most elections. We registered 75,000 black voters. We don't have enough votes to win a Congressional race, but we certainly can decide one. That is what we're going to be doing from now on.

When I drove home late one night during my race for Congress, a car circled my house. I keep guards around my house, and one of them, Cooper, was standing behind the bush by the driveway. The driver must have seen me. When the car shot, Cooper shot back. We escaped injury, but they hit one of my fence posts.

On another occasion the students over at Mississippi College said they wanted to hear me speak. This is an all-white Baptist college, one of the worst racist schools we've had, where blacks have never been able to do anything, not even work as a janitor. But the students said the least they could do was hear me. When I went there I was scared to death. I was so stiff when I came out on the stage that I could hardly walk. I had never been confronted with that many whites. But when I walked out on the stage the ovation I received was so shocking I was speechless for three or four minutes.

I have had other invitations to talk to young people in Mississippi. But the Board of Trustees of the Mississippi Institutions of Higher Learning had banned me from speaking at any state-supported college in the state. But, to show you how youngsters are changing, the white students at Mississippi State and Ole Miss protested formally by filing suit in the courts against the administration because they wouldn't let me come to speak. They won, and I spoke. The young whites are beginning to see that change must come, that their parents have been wrong.

24

The white police came into the church at Port Gibson in 1969 where we were organizing voter registration, and beat black folks and cursed the church, and that was one of the greatest mistakes they could have made. That was the one thing the racists did that really knitted us together. We immediately slapped a boycott on the whites until they paid for their sins.

Yes, white people burn our churches—they burned forty-two of them in the first five years after Medgar was killed. But in every community where they burned a church they brought us closer together. Because there's something about the church to us Southerners that means everything to us. That's the one place we knew we could go and be safe. Since 1965 the Hollywood Baptist Church in Fayette has been headquarters for our civil rights movement.

It's a Christian movement, a movement of nonviolence with positive, precise goals.

Blacks in Mississippi are getting tough. We better not catch our ministers not big enough for us. We don't want any Uncle Tom in our pulpit. We aren't going to pay him, that's all. If the pastor's not right, we kick him out. If he's right we get with him, and push him. When he slows up, we tighten up on him. We know how to tighten up on him: If he's receiving $100 a week, we cut him down to $75. Then when he does right, we loosen up on him, give him some more money. And we're tired of preachers, we need some pastors. A preacher is a man who goes to church once a week. You see him only on Sunday. A pastor is a man who teaches us on Sunday, he cares for the poor on Monday, he goes to the hospital on Tuesday, he's at the welfare office on Wednesday, and down to the sheriff's office on Thursday, and Friday wherever he's needed, and Saturday night he's in the honky-tonk talking to us. That's what we need.

We're tired of going to heaven on Sunday and can't get any work on Monday. We have to work every day. And we'll go to heaven when we don't have anywhere else to go. Nobody wants to go to heaven today, including the ministers. We mustn't fool ourselves. We've got to learn to live and help our folks.

My religion says one thing: *I want to be free.* We're not going to teach hate, white folks. We're just going to stop you from hating us. We're not going to beat you, white folks—and you better not try to kill us anymore.

I was down in Pike County trying to get Negroes to run for public office, and I was denounced publicly in the church by the pastor: "We don't need you here. You create trouble. And you're going to get us killed. You're going to get the rest of us fired. We got to get along with these white people." I'm talking about a town with seven hundred blacks and three hundred whites, and the blacks control nothing. I didn't get angry with the pastor. He's seventy years old and it's going to take time, patience and understanding to change his kind. When he told me they didn't want me back, I told him, "Brother, I understand. And I respect you for being afraid, because to kill a nigger in Mississippi ain't nothing. No one cares. And you have a right to be afraid. But you can't let your fears take away the things you must do. Your telling me not to come back is not really *you*. It's that you are afraid. I'm going to come back." And the following Sunday he led a song for us.

I'm going to do the best I can, but I'm not going to Tom around. An Uncle Tom is a guy who'll run back and tell the white people on other Negroes. He's the man who's grinning when he's not tickled—just grinning and scratching when he doesn't itch. The average Tom we know is that rascal who lays around, or sits around, watching us in our freedom movement and then runs to the white man. Yet it's sometimes necessary to do things in order to get a chance to do something better someplace else—it's like stalling for time.

My uncle Mark Thomas was what today's young liberals, black and white, call an Uncle Tom because he *yes sirred* and *no sirred* the white folks. But I could see how shrewd he was. He used a lot of psychology on white people. I think maybe I got some of mine from him, and my momma. Not from my daddy, because he was just brute force, he didn't stand for diplomacy or for sweet-talking any man. I think Uncle Mark shaped my life as far as business was concerned. He believed in having something of his own. And he didn't believe in working for anybody except himself.

Uncle Mark was the kind who could look a white man in the eye and tell him what he wanted to hear, and then do just the reverse. If a white man came to see him he'd say, "Good mornin'. Well, you're lookin' mighty fine today, sir." And the white man would think he was putting Uncle Mark in his pocket, and he'd tell Mark he was going to do such and such for him, or for his church, and Mark would smile and say, "Yes, sir. I sure appreciate that." Then the white man would want to gossip: "Well, Mark, what about Auntie Dorothy Lea? Is she really going with that white man?" or something like that, and Uncle Mark would say, "Well, you see, I don't know about that, but if I find out, I'll let you know, sir." Uncle Mark took advantage of white people, he played them for fools, and he got almost anything he wanted. He wasn't a *Tom*, but he played it real cool. He didn't go telling anything on anybody. So I don't worry too much when someone says, "He's an Uncle Tom." Let me tell you something. Down through the years, all of us, including Charles Evers, at one time had to do a little Uncle Toming. For our safety and security and survival. But I also make it clear to my people: You ain't going to say "yes, sir" and "no, ma'am" anymore to white folks. It's "yes" and "no." Don't go to any back door. That's inferiority when you go in there. And don't go to any doctor's office in the back door. There should be only one waiting room for patients.

25

The Democratic Party in New York is hardly the Democratic Party in Mississippi. I think the Democrats of Mississippi should find out where they stand. It's going to be up to the Democratic Party to make up its mind whether Eastland and Stennis are going to stay as Democrats or whether they are going to kick them out as Dixiecrats. In 1971 the Democrats are no longer in control of the executive branch, but they're not really out of control. We're still in the majority in both houses.

White people have a difficult time. When they decide they don't want to be racist, where do they go? They call some black man—like me—and cry on his shoulder. There's a white Mississippi attorney who calls me all the time and tells we what the racists are planning against me, how they are trying to turn the blacks against me. I'm for organizing the Democratic Party in this state and making it the party of all the people, for all those who want to come —not with the NAACP, but all those who are Democrats and want to come—the black and the white.

They are saying it's going to be an all-black party. Well, if it takes being an all-black party to make it right, let it be an all-black party. If because we want to be involved in our government, that's going to make it all black, get out, white folks, because we're going to stay in. If whites are that narrow, if they want to sit back and live for $50 a month and run those old run-down hospitals, and bow and scratch and grin to stay in a town so they can run it, well they're crazy. If they want to work with us, I'm with them. We anticipate a government that blacks and whites can participate in equally.

For all the black people's woes, I'm not blaming any particular *one*. I think all the white people are responsible some. And anyone could do a lot more if he would just say and do what is right. And the fellows with the pen could do a lot. The *Jackson Daily News,* the *Clarion Ledger* and the *Natchez Democrat* and the rest of the papers could change the whole attitude of this state.

If you have a political campaign for prices, you're not ever going to change this system. Once a man pays you off he doesn't owe you anything. If we start taking money because we support a candidate we'll never be able to straighten this out. Bobby never gave me a dime, but I loved him and campaigned for him all over. That's what bothers me about the average guy, he's so easy to buy off. They give us black people judgships, they give us these big titles—for example, I was offered Louis Martin's old job, deputy chairman of the Democratic National Committee. Something's always there—it's yours for the asking if you have any kind of voice at all. I want no part of it.

Some people are really our friends, but they don't have any blacks working for them. McGovern doesn't have any.

Teddy's got maybe one. Muskie doesn't know what a black man looks like, except what he sees on television. So what are they talking about?

A guy I really approve of is Senator Mondale, from Minnesota. He's got six or eight blacks working for him.

We don't like it that the Democratic Party is still funding and sending patronage to the state representatives and United States representatives and senators who have fought everything the Democratic Party is supposed to stand for. They have denounced every program that would be for all the people, regardless of color. Now we are getting people involved in policy-making and decision-making, the poor whites and the poor blacks. We involve a cross-section of people. Every time I go to Washington, I tell them, "The Democratic Party has taken the black vote for granted too long." They asked me to be on the Democratic National Committee, which decides the policies for the Democratic Party. It had been lily-white all these years, and suddenly they decided they wanted to put a black man on it. I didn't want to take it. I felt they were trying to tie my hands and shut my mouth up. I called Congressman Diggs and told him I wouldn't take it unless all the Democratic National Committee members and the Congressmen sent me a telegram saying they all wanted me. And even then I wasn't going to take it to be window dressing. I'm going to be heard. And if I'm not going to be heard I don't want the position without any authority. We've got enough black folks in positions without authority. After we discussed all this, I accepted their offer. The committee is made up of twelve people—and I'm the only black. I got news for them, though. They're going to know the problems and wishes of black folks. I'm going to give them facts. White people have a way of "honoring" Negroes out of their usefulness.

26

Martin Luther King and I were on practically every march together. He was often with me in my home in Jackson, and one time we had a big crowd and the womenfolks had the beds and the husbands all slept on the floor. I'll never forget that before the James Meredith march Martin came and spent a whole week with me. He said, "Charles, I'm nonviolent, but I feel safer when I'm around you than I do with anybody. I know you got plenty of guns and plenty of protection."

I've always believed Martin was killed because of a conspiracy. The only "proof" I have is my belief. If I had more I'd sure run to the authorities with it. The black people in this country know that John Kennedy and Bobby and Medgar and Martin were killed because of the system itself. It has created the kind of atmosphere, the kind of climate, that permits any man who differs with it to be killed—and the ones who have plotted their deaths to feel that they are doing what the majority of people want done and to feel that they should go unpunished. That's the kind of conspiracy I'm talking about. In Dr. King's case, I believe—and I'm almost sure—that there were men who raised money and paid Ray to do what he did, because Ray, as dumb as he is, didn't have the kind of connections to get across the country like he did without some help.

Now, anybody should know this, including the FBI— and tell them I said so. What we all know is that while Martin was killed, the spirit he inspired in others will always be among us.

During the peak of Martin's protest in Alabama, a group of us was in Selma trying to organize a march to get the Voter Registration Bill passed. On the particular Sunday the march was to begin, most of us—for some reason or another—just happened not to be there. Martin wasn't there. And I wasn't there either. And "Little John" Lewis led the group across the bridge. And when they got to the bridge the state troopers started beating them. They beat John down to the ground. He didn't do a thing, just lay there and rolled, and they beat him and beat him. He got up and staggered, and kept trying to go. They beat all those people who were there, and that's the Sunday they call the "Selma Bridge" Sunday. That really was the turning point for all of us. That's why I've said, "John Lewis above all is the one young man who stood firm and took the beatings and made it possible for us to build the kind of march that we had to Selma." Martin, whom I loved like a brother, got the credit, but I think too often people who really cause things to happen are never mentioned. And had it not been for John Lewis' courage that Sunday there never would have been a march. Because when John marched and they beat him, and the others with him, it generated the kind of enthusiasm, the kind of support, across the country that was needed. It was John Lewis who did it. Along with the people who followed him.

Look what happened to our black people down there in Birmingham. It was Sunday school, and they were praying, the racists blew their brains out. Dr. King never did anything against white folks. All he did was pray for them. Yet they shot his brains out. My people, you've got to understand this. Stop being scared. You're going to die sooner or later anyway. You're better off dead than living if you do nothing. You have to be concerned about your community, and your fellow man.

In the South they've gone from the Ku Klux Klan sheets to the policeman's badge. In the first five months of 1969 police killed five of our black folks, and it was called justifiable homicide. The good whites sat there, idly, and let it happen. All the merchants sit up there and let this sort of thing go on. They let the racists beat and kill Negroes who could represent 80 percent of their businesses. They kill them in the streets and give it no thought. So, you see, it makes the young people say, "Oh hell, it won't work. Let's tear it all down."

Port Gibson is about twenty miles north of Fayette. Like Fayette it's predominantly Negro. But it has always been ruled by racists. Until 1965 there were practically no blacks registered in Port Gibson—maybe one or two, but they didn't vote. We explained to the people the power they would have if only they voted. Then we told them that the economics of Port Gibson is 90 percent black because many of the whites don't trade in Port Gibson. So we slapped a boycott on them, and we held it for about six months, a tight boycott. It wasn't as tight as it should have been, but finally we got a few hired in stores, we got two policemen, we got one deputy sheriff, we got them to stop calling us "boy" and "girl" and police brutality was cut down. But we still didn't control anything. So what little money we had we spent with those who seemed to appreciate it. Then we began to push for other things—better schools, better streets, better sewers. The more we pushed, the more they resisted. They hired their city police chief from McComb, and they hired an assistant chief with a record of being mean and brutal to black people, and they hired a black policeman who was known to be a Tom. He was to spy on the black folks and intimidate them.

Things came to a head when this assistant chief and the black policeman went to arrest a young Negro. They said he had interfered with the arrest of another young black. In point of fact, he just asked them why they were arresting a man because he was drunk and why didn't they carry him home, and they didn't like this.

This white policeman had a record of beating Negroes, "smart niggers" he'd call them. And so he took the black Tom policeman to get the young Negro, and then the white policeman snatched the young boy off his porch (he weighed 145 pounds, the white policeman weighed 245 pounds, the black Tom policeman 216 pounds). The young black was unarmed—didn't even have a toothpick in his hand—and his wife and sister and two children were standing on the porch with him. They snatched him off the porch and the white policeman shot him through the stomach, then turned him loose and let him fall down in his own front yard before his wife, two children and sister, and let him lay there in his own blood forty-five minutes before they took him to the hospital where he was pronounced dead on arrival.

That night I was called at my house in Jackson about ten o'clock by one of our friends in Port Gibson. He said, "Mr. Evers, you'd better hurry and come down here because there's going to be trouble. They've just killed one

[177]

of our friends and the people are mad. They're up at the courthouse."

I said, "Get our people in the church. I'll be there." I jumped in the truck and took off down the Natchez Trace about ninety miles an hour, and in about an hour I was in Port Gibson. It was almost midnight. The whites had called out all the highway patrol and had deputized vigilantes, and they just beat every Negro on the street. They claimed some Negro threw a rock. *A rock!*

I rushed to the church, and it was full, and I saw all this commotion. Before I could get into the church there was a shot and one of the policemen fell and then they carried him out. I rushed in, I asked them to go home because they would be in more trouble with me among them. They had beaten Horace Lightfoot and any number of others half to death. Mr. Lightfoot was lying in a pool of blood. We finally got him to a hospital. We didn't know which of the patrolmen did it, so we said we were going to sue. Then they heard about this and they made out a warrant against him, saying Mr. Lightfoot had attacked them.

The man hadn't done a thing. They picked on him because he was the only Negro since Reconstruction that had been elected to the school board. They charged him with attempted assault and battery on a police officer and set his trial. I didn't want to go in the courtroom, because I didn't want to prejudice the jury, but I stayed nearby. Then one of the kids came running and said, "Mr. Evers, hurry, they're going to put Mr. Lightfoot in jail."

I got there when they were dismissing the jury and heard the city prosecutor say, "I want him arrested now." I said, "Your Honor, may I ask what's this about?"

The judge told me that Lightfoot didn't report to court for his hearing. I said, "Well, look here, the man can't, because he's in the hospital. He'll report. He's just sick.

You know, you broke his arm, you broke his ribs, you beat in his head, so he ain't able to come out. I assure you he'll come."

The prosecutor said, "He's supposed to be here in court. I want him now. I want him picked up. I want his arrest."

And I said, "Now, there's no point in arresting a man who's not able to move. I told you before, we'll get him here when he's able. All of you know Mr. Lightfoot. He's done all kinds of work for you, all of you, and you have no reason to think he's going to run off somewhere because of this. You know he's going to be here. Just give him a chance to get able and he'll be here."

The prosecutor repeated, "I said arrest him."

"Just remember," I said, "that someday the shoe is going to be on the other foot, and I hope you'll be able to wear it."

"Are you threatening me?"

"No, I'm telling you. Just remember, someday the shoe is going to be on the other foot, so be able to wear it."

"Are you threatening me?"

"I'm just telling you." He kept talking about me threatening him, and I said, "By the way, you don't run the court. That's the judge's job, not yours. You're just the prosecuting attorney hired by the city of Port Gibson. You do what the alderman and the mayor say, and you don't come here and tell us what to do. I'm asking the judge. Can we leave him out till he gets better, Your Honor? I'll see that he gets to court. Just give him a pass today."

Then the prosecutor jumped up and said, "You're interfering with me. You shut up!"

"You don't tell me to shut up. Who do you think you are, telling me to shut up? You're just a two-bit attorney. You ain't no judge, you ain't nothing. So you don't tell me to shut up."

Then he turned to the judge and shouted, "Arrest him! I want him arrested!"

"Arrest me for what? What are you going to arrest me for?"

"Arrest him for disturbing the peace."

I said, "I've been in jail many times for worse than that. But, man, who you think you're kidding? What peace did I disturb? *Your* peace? You don't need to arrest me, put those handcuffs on me. I'll go to jail." Then I said to the attorney, "Just remember, you might be coming to Fayette one day. . . ."

"You're threatening me again!"

"Attorney, you talk too much."

"Get your black ass on out of here, right now, damn it!"

That's when I said, "Now, wait a minute. Arrest him, chief. I want right now to swear out a warrant for his arrest, for insubordination, disrespect toward an American citizen—that's me—profane language in a public courtroom and disturbing the peace. I want him arrested right now."

The police chief's eyes were just popping, and he looked at me and then at the attorney, and he said, "What about that?"

And I replied, "He ain't got nothing to say. I'm asking you to arrest him. I'm swearing out a warrant for his arrest." And I signed a warrant for his arrest. Then the chief turned around and filled out my warrant and turned around and arrested the city prosecuting attorney.

Then the judge said to me, "You're on a $75 bail."

I said, "I ain't paying it, because I haven't done anything."

Then the judge said to the attorney, "Are you ready to go?"

"No, I'm going to put up my bond."

So he posted $125 bond and went on out, but they carried me to jail. Then the crowd began to build up and the police chief came around and said, "We're going to release you. We want to get you out of here."

So I said, "If it's going to save the town, I'll go." And then I told him, "Because we've got other ways to get the town."

So they let me out. I guess I'll hear the trial sometime. That's just one of the mockeries of the white man's justice.

27

On September 9, 1969, Fayette police arrested a white man, a former Ku Klux Klan leader, on charges of trying to kill me. The first tip came from a woman, it sounded like a white woman. She said, "Charles, I don't believe in everything that you do, but I can't see you killed. The Klan's going to try to kill you when you move that monument." This was the granite monument we'd put up to honor Medgar, and the whites forced us to move it from the county-owned park across the street to the city-hall grounds. I ignored her warning and laughed it off, but that evening a man called and told me the same thing, and I said, "The monument was moved this morning. Why are they going to kill me now? That's what they wanted, wasn't it? The monument moved?" I said, "I got things to do," and hung up. But then I began to worry. I had gotten calls before, sometimes one and two a day, but they didn't sound so exact. So I went and told the police, "Look, I've got some calls that some guy is going to try to kill me. Just sort of see if there's anyone strange around." Then I went on down to the store and told my daughter Pat about it.

"Daddy, we've been seeing some strange cars around here."

"Yeah? Well, just keep your eye on 'em."

At seven-fifteen that evening the phone rang again, and a female voice said, "Mister Evers, I'm a friend of yours. Now, don't hang up on me. . . ."

"Look, honey, what is it?"

"There's three men going to kill you."

"Aw, c'mon now."

"They're driving a 1968 Mustang. They've got five guns in the car. They've been on the road and bought some clothes for a quick change. And one of them is in Natchez in a motel, with a getaway car."

When they get that exact, you sort of listen again. Then she said, "And they got a rebel flag on the car." Well, I had seen that car. And then it hit me that what she was saying was for real, so I said, "Thank you very much." I believe this was a Negro woman—a Negro woman who was working for some white woman, possibly that same white woman who had called that morning. The white woman might have asked her husband to call, and when he wouldn't do it she got this Negro woman to call. Then I really got busy. Later on my daughter Carolyn came and told me, "Daddy, I saw that car, and the man came in the store and bought a piece of gum."

"We'll take care of it."

At about 7:40 P.M. I got my papers together and left the store and stopped in front of the restaurant to talk to some people. Carolyn was with me. She was sticking right with me. She said, "Look out, Daddy, here comes that car now!" And she jumped in front of me.

"Don't you get in front of me," I said. "I'll take care." And I had my gun. Then I saw the police had already spotted him. They were right behind him, and I made a motion to the police, sort of pointed to the car, and told them to get him. What threw us off was there was only one man in the car. But he had the five guns. The police got him and brought him on to city hall. I went there, and they brought him in to where I was.

The policeman said, "Mister Mayor, this man was speeding. We stopped him and found several guns in his car."

And I said to the man, "Don't you know it's against the law to carry all those guns in your car?"

And he said, "Ain't none of your business."

"Don't you know it's against the law to speed in this town, that there's an ordinance against speeding?"

"I wasn't speeding!"

"Before you say anything to me, remember now, I'm the judge and I'm the Mayor of the town, and whatever you say may come against you, so you can call your lawyer if you want to."

And he said, "You must remember that I'm a white man."

At that moment I came to know that I'm a good man, and I know I've been converted, because I would have knocked his teeth down his throat had it been three years earlier. I flinched when he said that, and I swore I wouldn't let him provoke me. Then I said, "Lock him up."

This guy had come to kill me. He almost admitted that. Later on he said to me, "You're fair. But I hate you."

I said, "Listen, T_____, I don't know your story. But why don't you and I just sit down and talk about it?"

"I don't want to talk about it!" But he was scared. His lawyer was there.

I said, "Listen, you don't know me and I don't know you. And what is all this? Why would you want to kill me? I don't want to kill you. I had all the chance in the world to kill you and I didn't kill you. Now, why would you want to kill me?" And the guy had to drop his head, he didn't know what to say. But, you see, he had never had this kind of talk before. He had been told that Evers was a big, black, smart nigger who's looking for power. But now he has a different opinion of me. He may kill me someday, but he has a helluva different opinion of me now than when he came down to Fayette. We had a hearing a couple of days later and I wouldn't even sit as judge because I wanted to make sure he had a fair trial. The mayor pro tem, who's my assistant, was authorized to hear the case. And we let the white man get his lawyer. We had picked up the other two men in the meantime. We had all the guns on display and we bound them over to the grand jury, which met a week later. We put them on a $10,000 bond. He wouldn't pay it, so he stayed in jail for five or six days. The grand jury didn't have enough evidence to hold him, so they turned him loose. Then the federal government grabbed him for violation of the Firearms Act. He never told me why he had those guns, but somebody said he told the FBI that he would get me at a later date. Somebody said he said, "I'm full of that Evers nigger up to my head," and, "I'm not going to stand any more of that smart-alecky nigger Mayor."

The reason why we've tightened up on my security is that somebody said they heard somebody say, "We know we can't get Evers in Fayette, but we'll get him on one of these trips he makes." And it's quite possible they've hired some nut in Washington or Philadelphia. Wherever you go, you can always find some gun for hire. But I've always felt—and Medgar, too—that it's not important when you die, or how long you live. The important thing is what you do while you're here. And I know Medgar made a contribution, and I'm trying to make one. And if I should go, well, there'll be someone else to take on and keep going. I can't go around worrying about when I'm going to die.

28

Mississippi is different from any other state in the nation. And despite the hate, the harassment, the intimidation, with all of its poor and the denial of basic human rights, there's still something about the state that we all love. There's something about the mean white people and the scary Negroes, there's a relationship between them that does not exist anyplace else. Yes, there's a closeness that exists between the Mississippi whites and blacks that doesn't exist elsewhere. I can't explain it.

When I went around campaigning for Mayor, I knew there were many blacks who were going to vote for my white opponent. It's one of those can't-explain things, but it's there. I don't think any white person can explain why Mississippi is so unique. Maybe it's because 90 percent of us, white and black, are poor people.

I've been asked by a lot of people, why I don't go to

New York or Chicago? Well, it's very simple why I stay in Mississippi. It's home. It's where my Momma and Daddy were born and bred and died, and my grandparents. It's where all of my friends are. I don't know any "home" other than here. Mississippi is also more conducive to living. I like the atmosphere, the open spaces, with plenty of land and fresh air. Of course, there's no jobs, but we're going to make jobs. I honestly believe that here in Mississippi there's a better future. Moreover, in Mississippi a man knows better where he stands. We know the hatemonger and the bigot, we know the klansman, the racist, the murderer. We know him by name, we know all about him—and we can deal with him. Once we get him under control we'll be able to enjoy the things here that every other American has a right to enjoy. But in the North you don't have that chance. They look at you and pat you on the back, then they stab you in the back.

We know that once we can end racial hatred in Mississippi it's going to be the best place to live because there's a closeness between black and white, and it's there even now, although, as I've said, none of us can understand it. It's a relationship that—bad as it may have been socially and otherwise—we all know is there. I guess we all know about it because when a black person gets sick the white people in Mississippi—most of them—seem to care, and they go see about that sick person, even if they treated him badly.

Now, Harlem is the worst place in America for black folks. You might say Adam Clayton Powell's done a few things. But Powell could have done a helluva lot more. I'm going to fix Fayette up, if nothing else. You've got to fix up home. I couldn't care less what happens to other parts of the country right now. I've got to get Fayette right. That's all I'm saying. I can't go to New York and tell you what's good for New York, or what's good for Washington.

Powell has finally realized he's a Negro. For a long time he thought he was white. He acted like white folks, he talked like white folks, he associated with white folks, but he finally realized he's a Negro. He owns ghetto houses, and he owns houses he won't rent to Negroes. Our problem has been: We've rarely had a black man we could trust. We've rarely had a black man who would tell the truth.

It's still unbelievable to me how free black people have been in Harlem all these years to register, how easy it's been. But I've found out that most black people in Harlem *aren't* registered. They don't seem to care. And what they've got to understand is that there's no cause to riot if you can vote. I don't care how much you riot, how much you pray—that white man fears only one thing: your power to replace one official with another by the ballotbox. I was surprised when I got to Harlem to find out that there were only 27 percent of the qualified black folk who were registered. This is *unbelievable*. Now, these folks have been privileged to register all of their lives. My argument with them is that I don't want to hear how black and proud you are. *Get out there and prove it*. And you only prove it by getting organized and voting.

I first found out about voter registration in the ghetto when I was campaigning for John Kennedy in 1960 and for Bobby Kennedy in 1964. And ever since then I've been going to Harlem and finding out that they're just not ready, they're not organized. And the same way on the West Side of Chicago and the South Side of Chicago. If they'd only get together and get organized they could change things. Another thing that surprised me in Harlem was that 99 percent of the businesses there are owned by white people. The Negroes are running around and saying, "I'm black and proud," but they don't own anything, they don't control any political jobs or anything. They're only fooling themselves. Somebody's got to get in there and show the importance of the vote.

We've marched and we've knocked down the walls of segregation preventing us from going into restaurants and hotels and motels, but now we've got to knock down the wall that keeps us from getting enough money to go in there—that economic and political wall. And once you can control your politics, your economics will come. I talked to any number of Harlem leaders and all they'd say to me was, "Well, you just don't understand." The ordinary Negroes told me they never saw their so-called political leaders unless it was election time. The leaders weren't really a part of the community, and some of them were doing the same thing that whites have done—just using them.

29

Jackson, Mississippi, 1970

What happened at Jackson State College on the night of May 14, 1970, was a case of students acting as students and Mississippi police acting as murderers. The college has about four thousand black students. My daughter Sheila was in school there. The students were upset about the invasion of Cambodia by American troops and about the draft for the armed services, but that was only part of it. The students know only too well that down here they translate what you call "conservatism" into nigger-killing. The police went to the campus and killed two black youngsters and wounded twelve others. The day of killing Negroes is gone. I've preached nonviolence because I don't think blacks can win the other way, but there comes a time when a man doesn't care anymore about winning.

Somehow a rumor got started at Jackson State College that white policemen had murdered me, and this really set the students off. There had been a little disturbance the night before, so I went out to the campus. I talked to the kids and told them, "Now, cool it, because these bigots will kill you. They're murderers, they killed my brother, they killed Bobby, they killed Martin, they killed John, and the same kind of *ism* that killed them will kill you." And most of them promised me they were going to cool it. That same night I took a plane to go to Walter Reuther's funeral. I was going to Detroit, but we ran into bad weather, so I had to stop in Chicago. The next morning I was at the airport to catch an eight o'clock flight to Detroit when I saw a couple of newsmen running down the corridor: "Hey, Charles! What are you doing here? We just heard you got killed."

"Oh, get out of here. What you mean, I got killed? You see me, don't you?"

And one said, "No, we just heard you got killed."

"Oh, come on. I hear this all the time. I'm not dead. Feel me."

Then about five more rushed up, and Hugh Hill, who was with CBS in Chicago, looked at me all funny and said, "Charles, we heard some whites had shot you."

And I said, "What are you guys talking about?"

And he said, "They killed two blacks in Jackson last night."

"You must be out of your mind," I said. But when I phoned home, my daughter Sheila screamed, "Oh, Daddy, thank God you're safe."

"What is it, Sheila? What's wrong with you?"

And she said, "They said you had been shot." Then she said, "Daddy, don't come back."

Then my wife took the phone, and she was in a rage. She told me someone had driven through the campus and told the students that I had been shot, and that the kids started protesting, and that highway patrolmen came in and killed two kids. I don't know how the rumor got started, but it was unnecessary to mow down innocent people. If there was a sniper up there, go get the sniper. The way the highway patrol explained it was all a lie. The little Gibbs boy had on his tuxedo and had just walked his sister home from the prom. Now, you ain't really hardly going to find a boy in his tuxedo out there shooting a pistol. And the little Green boy was just coming home from a 40¢-an-hour job at a restaurant and was on the other side of the street, walking along and trying to dodge the bullets. I'm sure he didn't know what was going on. But they turned and shot him down—for no reason. This is the kind of hatred and racism we've lived with all these years. The whites even claimed it was the blacks doing the shooting. This kind of whitewash is going on in Jackson and other places where blacks and whites have gotten together to try to end this hate. And when something happens to this group, it's all over. It's like when Medgar was killed the FBI came in to question me and said they had reason to believe that I killed him—and I was in Chicago the night he was killed. I threw them out of my office, quick. It's the kind of whitewash the blacks have suffered over the years, and I can understand blacks being angry.

30

Dear Medgar,

We miss you. And I especially miss you. I had always figured that you and I would wind up together fighting against all the things that seemed to dehumanize our men and women and children. But, somehow, I left you alone too soon in the fight. You had just gotten started in the civil rights movement and I went up North to make money. It was you who stuck it out here in Mississippi, you who gave our people a voice, you who told the white folks what had to be done to make this country a happy place for all of us to live. You fought without me.

I'll never forgive myself for letting you battle alone. When we were kids, we always double-teamed to take on the bullies. And when we did we were invincible. When you took on the Klan, the White Citizens Council, and began laying down the law to the haters, I was far from the battlefield.

Well, Medgar, things have changed. And I have changed.

And our folks are changing, too. We're starting to double-team on racism. What's happening would really do you proud. We have our people in every single public school in this state. We have black policemen in almost every town. Little by little, we're having a say in the education of Mississippi's youth. You see black faces every day on television news programs. Asking questions and supplying answers.

There are lots of little things that we take for granted now. Things that you fought for, things that Momma and Daddy never dreamed would happen in Mississippi in a hundred years. For example, nobody tells us we can't use a gas station washroom any more. And nobody gets tried without having at least one black man on the jury. Finally, the Federal Government has begun to keep an eye on the rascals and keep them in line. Sure, they kick up sand now and then. But, Medgar, we've got them on the run.

It's hard for me to express this just right. But the black folks of Mississippi know that the progress we've made we owe to you, and to the spirit that drove you and Martin and Bobby and others. You're with us every step of the way. Never an NAACP meeting is held, or a church meeting goes on, or a political conversation takes place that we don't hear "Medgar this" and "Medgar that."

One thing you were worried about, I know, was that black people might, in their frustration, take to guns and violence. There are extremists, mostly up North, who have tried that route. Nobody's really fooled by haters. We've proven here in Mississippi what *does* work: brotherhood, patience, courage, firmness of purpose, organization, the ballotbox, intelligence.

When you died, I was tempted to take a foolish course, to start avenging your death by "getting even." It would have been so easy to do away with the racists, one by one. I even brought guns down from Chicago to do the job. Thank the Lord, I didn't go through with that madness.

I'm especially thankful because we've created something truly beautiful. Your big brother is the Mayor of Fayette. Imagine, Medgar, we black folks actually control and govern and live happily in a bi-racial town in the State of Mississippi.

[195]

And it's your example that's steering us right: playing fair with one and all, white and black. I've learned how important it is for the community leader to crack down whenever bigotry or bullying occur. I'm as firm with my folks as Daddy was with us. In Fayette you'll see something different in the people, something perky in the way they look at you, a kind of energy in their stride. The old hangdog look has gone. Now you see hope, you see friendliness, you see enthusiasm.

Remember, Medgar, when that old Bilbo warned that rabble if they weren't careful they'd wake up to find those two little nigger boys representing them? Well, he wasn't far wrong. We are representing them, quite a few of them. And the craziest thing of all, Medgar, is that now that they know us they kind of like us.

Love,
Charles